H. R. Meck has extensive industrial experience and has published a number of journal articles primarily in the field of solid mechanics.

PRENTICE-HALL, INC. Englewood Cliffs, N.J. 07632

A SPECTRUM BOOK

H.R. MECK

SCIENTIFIC ANALYSIS FOR PROGRAMMABLE CALCULATORS*

PROGRAMMING TECHNIQUES, SCIENCE AND ENGINEERING APPLICATIONS

*WITH ALGEBRAIC OPERATING SYSTEMS

Library of Congress Cataloging in Publication Data

Meck, H. R.
  Scientific analysis for programmable calculators.

  (A Spectrum Book)
  Bibliography: p.
  Includes index.
   1. Programmable calculators.   2. Mathematics—Data processing.   3. Science—Mathematics—Data
processing.   4. Engineering mathematics—Data processing.   I. Title.
QA75.M36   510'.28'542   80–26677
ISBN 0–13–796417–X
ISBN 0–13–796409–9 (pbk.)

Editorial/production supervision and interior design by Cyndy Lyle
Manufacturing buyer Barbara Frick

Prentice-Hall International, Inc., *London*
Prentice-Hall of Australia Pty. Limited, *Sydney*
Prentice-Hall of Canada, Ltd., *Toronto*
Prentice-Hall of India Private Limited, *New Delhi*
Prentice-Hall of Japan, Inc., *Tokyo*
Prentice-Hall of Southeast Asia Pte. Ltd., *Singapore*
Whitehall Books Limited, *Wellington, New Zealand*

CONTENTS

2

ROOTS OF EQUATIONS 37

3

SOME HIGHER TRANSCENDENTAL FUNCTIONS 55

4

NUMERICAL INTEGRATION   81

5

DIFFERENTIAL EQUATIONS   113

APPENDIX

PREFACE

This book is concerned with scientific programming for a large core programmable calculator. Although calculators of this type have become extremely popular in the past few years, it has been my observation that most units are used for rather elementary problems that do not take advantage of their full capacity. With suitable programming, a pocket calculator can be used to solve many moderately complicated scientific problems usually assigned to a full-sized computer. To the best of my knowledge, until now there has been no book that fully exploits this capability. This book fills that gap. A pocket calculator is often much more convenient than a computer, because an engineer or student can run a calculation at any time and obtain results immediately without waiting for access to a computer laboratory.

There are two types of programmable calculator. RPN (reverse Polish notation) calculators are manufactured by Hewlett-Packard. AOS (algebraic operating system) calculators are manufactured by Texas Instruments and a number of other companies. A discussion of the various models is in reference 14. The programs in this book are written for the TI-58/58C/59 calculator, but they can easily be adapted to run on any other AOS calculator, provided that the capacity of the calculator is great enough.* They can also be adapted to run on an RPN calculator, although this may require a substantial amount of work for some programs.

This book explains useful programming techniques and can be used as a text for readers who wish to develop some skill in writing programs. It also serves as a convenient reference book, because the programs are useful in themselves and can be applied to practical problems. Answers are given for virtually all problems. Suggested solutions are given at the back of the book for the more difficult problems. Like the text, the problems can be used either for learning or for reference, since a number of the solved problems are of practical interest.

Chapter 1 presents the most important statements and solves a number of representative problems. Chapter 2 is concerned with finding roots of equations, and Chapter 3 evaluates a number of commonly occurring transcendental functions. Chapter 4 is devoted to numerical integration, and Chapter 5 is concerned with differential equations. If the book is used as a text, Chapter 1 should be read first. (However, the material in section 5 on Legendre polynomials and the material in section 6 on Lagrange interpolation and sorting numbers may be omitted on the first reading.) The remaining four chapters are almost entirely independent of one another and may be read in any order. If the book is used for reference, programs of interest can be extracted from any part of the book without studying the background material.

The emphasis throughout the book is on programming, not on the theoretical foundations of numerical analysis. However, derivations of the most important numerical methods are given in an appendix.

A comment on the choice of material is desirable. This book will probably be used primarily with the TI-58/59 calculator. Two manuals and a program library (references 1 and 2) are supplied with this calculator; every owner has these. This material covers a few aspects of scientific programming well, but most aspects are treated perfunctorily or omitted entirely. In writing this book it seemed desirable to concentrate on topics largely neglected in the manuals. A few topics covered well in the manuals or program library (e.g., matrices and simultaneous equations) have been omitted from this book. However, there is a discussion in Chapter 1, section 7, that calls attention to the material furnished with the calculator and shows how it can

---

* The TI-58 and 58C are identical except that the 58C has continuous memory. In this book both models are referred to simply as the TI-58.

be used, either by itself or in conjunction with the material of this book.

There is a strong element of personal choice in writing programs, and any book reflects some particular viewpoint. No matter what approach is adopted, it is probably inevitable that some readers will find that some of their favorite techniques have been neglected. The programming techniques used in this book differ in some respects from those used in the TI manual (reference 1). The manual (and most other books on programming) emphasizes the use of flow charts as aids to writing programs. In my opinion, the value of this technique is greatly overrated. The total amount of effort required to prepare a flow chart and program is much greater than that required to write the program directly. The preparation of a good flow chart requires a considerable amount of time and effort, and even after it is completed it does not significantly decrease the time required to write the program. A different technique is used in this book. The programs are written in short segments. Each segment, which appears as a horizontal line, performs a specific function within the program. Each program is accompanied by comments to explain the function of each line. I believe that this technique is easier to use and more efficient than the flow chart approach. A similar format has been used in reference 13. However, any reader who wishes to do so may draw his own flow charts.

Two other differences between this book and reference 1 may be mentioned. In this book we generally avoid the use of multiple levels of parentheses; the equal sign is used instead, leading to shorter programs and also tending to decrease the probability of error (Chapter 1, section 1). Also, labels are used more sparingly in this book than in reference 1; excessive use of labels tends to increase program running time with little or no gain in ease of operation (Chapter 1, section 5).

I assume that the reader is familiar with undergraduate engineering mathematics and with the ordinary keyboard operation of a scientific calculator. I also assume that the reader has the manufacturer's manuals supplied with the programmable calculator. The amount of effort necessary to learn the material of this book depends to some extent on the reader's background. A reader with prior knowledge of computer programming can learn calculator programming very easily, because the most important elements (e.g., conditional transfers, loops, subroutines) are similar. For a reader with no prior knowledge of programming of any kind, somewhat greater effort may be necessary. However, there is a compensating benefit. Anyone who has mastered calculator programming can easily learn computer programming if this becomes necessary later.

SCIENTIFIC ANALYSIS FOR PROGRAMMABLE CALCULATORS

1

INTRODUCTION

In this chapter we consider a number of problems which are of interest in themselves and also illustrate several important programming techniques. It is assumed that the reader is familiar with the ordinary keyboard operation of a scientific calculator. It is also assumed that the reader has access to a manual for a programmable calculator, which gives detailed information on the operation of the programming keys. The programs in this book are written for the TI Programmable 58/59 calculator, but can be adapted to other models.

1. Polynomials

As a simple example of programming, we consider the problem of evaluating the polynomial

$$y = 3 - 5x + 2x^2 + x^3 \tag{1}$$

The most efficient way to evaluate this is to start by writing it in nested form as

$$y = 3 + x(-5 + x(2 + x)) \tag{2}$$

We have used parentheses only instead of parentheses and brackets in order to make the algebraic equation look as much as possible like the program equation. The program is

```
0   LRN                                                      000

1   3 + RCL01 × (5+/− + RCL01 × (2 + RCL01)) =
    R/S                                                      021


    LRN
```

The input/output operation is

```
Press   x   STO01   RST   R/S

Display                    y
```

The LRN statement puts the calculator into the learn (program) mode. If it is already in the learn mode, it returns it to keyboard operation. Hence the line between the two LRN statements constitutes the program. In the input operation, the numerical value of x is stored in data register 01. The RST (reset) statement moves the program pointer to program location number 000. (The program location number is the three digit number which appears in the calculator display at each step of the program, and is shown at the right of the above program.) The R/S (run/stop) statement starts the program running. The program is straightforward; it corresponds closely to the algebraic equation (2). The statement RCL01 recalls the numerical value of x from data register 01, where it has been stored. The R/S statement in the program, which occurs when the program is running, stops the execution and causes the current result of the calculation to be displayed. Numerical results for several values of x are given below.

x	−2	−1	0	1	2	3	4
y	13	9	3	1	9	33	79

The use of multiple levels of parentheses in a program is inefficient and often leads to errors. Simpler and more compact programs can be written by using the equal sign instead of parentheses. The evaluation begins with the expression inside the innermost parentheses. With this technique, the program for equation (2) becomes

0   LRN   000

1   RCL01 + 2 = × RCL01 − 5 = × RCL01 + 3 = R/S   018

    LRN

The input/output operation is the same as before, i.e.

Press   x   STO01   RST   R/S

Display   y

It is not necessary to have the RCL01 statement at the beginning of the program; the parameter x is in the display register when the program starts running. The program can be simplified to

0   LRN   000

1   + 2 = × RCL01 − 5 = × RCL01 + 3 = R/S   016

    LRN

The input/output operation is still unchanged.

The parameter x must still be stored, because it is recalled later in the program. However, this can be done as well in the program as in the input. We rewrite the program as

0   LRN   000

1   STO01 + 2 = ×RCL01− 5 = × RCL01 + 3 = R/S   018

    LRN

This program is two steps longer than the preceding one, but the input/output operation is simplified to

Press   x   RST   R/S

Display   y

This program is more convenient than the preceding ones because it has a very simple input. The program is punched into the calculator only once, but the input is inserted repeatedly for each required value of x.

We consider one final version of the program:

0   LRN   000

1   STO01 + 2 = × RCL01 − 5 = × RCL01 + 3 = R/S
    RST   019

    LRN

The input for the first calculation is still x RST R/S. However, subsequent results are obtained by simply pressing x R/S. The RST statement at the end of the program resets the program pointer automatically at the beginning of each subsequent evaluation.

2. Conditional transfers; discontinuous functions

It is often necessary to evaluate a function which is given by one formula over one part of an interval and by a different formula over another part of the interval. The conditional transfer statements

$x \rightleftharpoons t$, 2nd $x \geq t$ are used for problems of this type. Consider the function

$$y = 1, \ x < 0 \qquad y = x + 2, \ x \geq 0 \qquad (3)$$

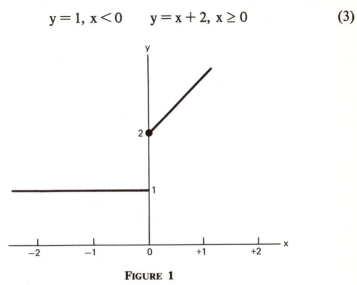

FIGURE 1

which is sketched in Fig. 1. The program is

0	LRN	000

1   STO01   0 x $\rightleftharpoons$ t   RCL01   2nd x $\geq$ t 012
    1 = R/S   012

2   +2 = R/S   016

    LRN

The input/output operation is

Press   x   RST   R/S

Display   y

The statement STO01 stores the value of x in data register 01. The statement $0 \ x \rightleftharpoons t$ puts the number 0 into the display register and then transfers it to the test register. The statement RCL01 brings the numerical value of x into the display register. The conditional transfer statement 2nd $x \geq t$ 012 compares the value of x in the display register with the number 0 in the test register. If $x \geq 0$, the execution of the program moves on to program location number 012. The next statements, + 2 =, add 2 to the value of x which is in the display register. The R/S statement stops the execution of the program and displays the result, x + 2. Returning to line 1, suppose that x < 0. Then the conditional transfer statement 2nd x ≥ t 012 has no effect. The execution of the program continues to the next step. The number 1 is inserted into the display register. The R/S statement then stops the execution of the program and displays the result. Some numerical results are shown below.

x	−2	−1	0	1	2	3
y	1	1	2	3	4	5

In the example of Fig. 1, the transition point at x = 0 is on the right branch of the curve. We now consider the modified problem of Fig. 2. This represents the function

$$y = 1, \; x \leq 0 \qquad y = x + 2, \; x > 0$$

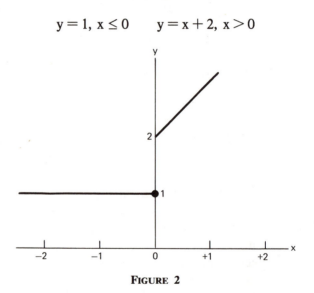

FIGURE 2

The transition point is now on the left branch. There is no x ≤ t key on the calculator. The desired comparison is carried out by again using the x ≥ t statement, but interchanging the roles of x and t. The program appears below. It is slightly shorter than the first program.

0　LRN   000

1　x ⇌ t　 0 2nd x ≥ t 010　 x ⇌ t + 2 = R/S　 010

LRN

The input/output operation is the same as the one for the first program. The numerical results are also the same, except that y = 1 when x = 0.

When a curve has two branches, it very often happens that the two branches meet at the transition point with no jump. In this case the transition point may be included in either branch, and either of the two foregoing approaches may be used.

Now suppose that the transition point is between the two branches, say y = 1.5 at x = 0. Then it is necessary to use two comparison statements: x = t and x ≥ t. The program follows.

0   LRN   000

1   x ⇌ t   0 2nd x = t 016   2nd x ≥ t 013   x ⇌ t + 2
        = R/S   013

2   1 = R/S   016

3   1.5 = R/S   021

LRN

The input/output operation is the same as the one used for the first program. The numerical results are also the same, except that y = 1.5 when x = 0.

When a curve has a finite discontinuity and the transition point is midway between the two branches, it is possible to use the signum function instead of a conditional transfer. The signum function is defined as follows:

$$\text{sgn } x = 1 \qquad x > 0$$
$$= 0 \qquad x = 0$$
$$= -1 \qquad x < 0$$

With the signum function, the equation for y becomes

$$y = \frac{1}{2}[x + 3 + (x + 1)\, \text{sgn}x]$$

7

The statement for the signum function is 2nd Op10. The program now becomes

        0   LRN   000

        1   STO01 + 1 = × RCL01 2nd Op10 + RCL01 + 3 =
            ÷ 2 = R/S   020

            LRN

The input/output operation is the same as the one for the first program.

It is sometimes necessary to write a program for a periodic function. Before proceeding with this problem, it is desirable to introduce the 2nd Int and INV 2nd Int statements. The Int (integer) statement discards the part of the number in the display register to the right of the decimal point; the INV Int statement discards the part to the left of the decimal point. These statements are useful in a number of applications.

Consider the periodic function sketched in Fig. 3. This represents the equation

$$y = x + 1 \qquad 0 \leq x < 2$$

and is repeated indefinitely in the direction of positive x. The program is

        0   LRN   000

        1   ÷ 2 = INV 2nd Int × 2 + 1 = R/S   RST   012

            LRN

        Input/output

        Press   x   RST   R/S

        Display   y

For results after the first, we press x R/S.

The foregoing program does not work if x is negative. If results are needed for negative values of x, the simplest procedure is to add

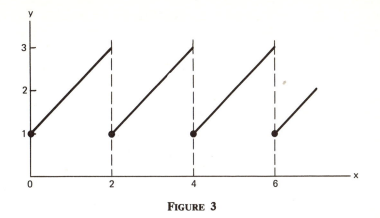

some large integer to x/2 before using the INV Int statement. The following program is valid for any $x \geq -2000$.

```
0   LRN                                                     000

1   ÷ 2 + 1000 = INV 2nd Int × 2 + 1 = R/S   RST      017

    LRN
```

If the transition points are not on the branches of the curve to the right of the discontinuities as shown in Fig. 3, the foregoing programs must be modified by using the x = t statement as discussed earlier.

3. The Dsz statement

The Dsz (decrement and skip on zero) statement is another conditional transfer statement. It is useful in a great many applications. To introduce this statement we consider the problem of finding the sum of the first n integers, that is, we evaluate the sum

$$S = 1 + 2 + 3 + \ldots + n \tag{4}$$

The program is

```
0   LRN                                                     000

1   ST001   0 ST002                                         005
```

9

2	RCL01	SUM02	009
3	2nd Dsz 1005		013
4	RCL02	R/S	016
	LRN		

Contents of data registers

01 n, n − 1, n − 2, ... , 1   02 partial sum n + (n − 1) + ...

Input/output

Press   n   RST   R/S

Display   S

Line 1 stores n in data register 01 and clears data register 02, which will contain the partial sum of the series. Line 2 recalls n and adds it to the content of data register 02. The Dsz statement in line 3 subtracts 1 from the number in data register 01 (the first of the four digits following the Dsz statement) and compares the result with zero. If it is greater than zero, the execution of the program is transferred to program location 005 (the last three of the four digits following the Dsz statement). Then lines 2 and 3 are repeated. The cycle is executed n times. The number in data register 01 is n for the first cycle, n-1 for the second cycle, n-2 for the third cycle, . . , 1 for the last cycle. The n cycles constitute a loop. After the n cycles are completed, the number in data register 02 is equal to the sum S. Line 4 recalls and displays the result. We observe that the series is summed from right to left. It is also clear that only the single digit data registers 0 through 9 can be used to hold the counter for a Dsz loop. We consider the numerical example n = 50. Then the result is S = 1275.

We mention that the 0 STO02 instruction in line 1 can be omitted and the program will still run correctly, provided that line 3 is changed to 2nd Dsz 1002. However, if the program is then used again with other values of n, the results will be incorrect unless the data registers are cleared each time. If the first entry into data register 02 (or any other data register) is a SUM instruction, any data left over from an earlier calculation will remain in the calculator and affect the current result.

In exactly the same way we write a program to evaluate the factorial

$$n! = n(n-1)(n-2) \ldots . 1 \qquad (5)$$

The program is

0	LRN	000
1	ST001 1 ST002	005
2	RCL01 2nd Prd 02	009
3	2nd Dsz 1005	013
4	RCL02 R/S	016
	LRN	

Contents of data registers

01 n, n − 1, ... , 1   02 n(n − 1) . . . .

Input/output

Press   n   RST   R/S

Display   n!

The only thing new is the Prd (product) statement in line 2. This multiplies the number in data register 02 by the number in the display register.

It is not necessary to store the partial product in each cycle. The program can be rewritten a little more concisely as follows:

0	LRN	000
1	ST001 1	003
2	× RCL01 = 2nd Dsz 1003 R/S	012
	LRN	

The foregoing programs break down when n = 0. This difficulty often occurs when a Dsz loop is used; the cycle always runs at least once before counting begins, even if n = 0. When a program is used alone to evaluate n!, this does not matter much; we do not need a program to find that 0! = 1. However, a program of this type is sometimes used as a segment in some more complicated program in which the case n = 0 may not be trivial.* In this case the program should be valid for any integral value of n ≥ 0. There are several possible ways to accomplish this. One way is to consider the case n = 0 separately by using a conditional transfer.† However, a simpler procedure is to use the fact that n! = (n + 1)!/(n + 1). Then the program becomes

0   LRN   000

1   + 1 = STO01 $\dfrac{1}{x}$ 006

2   × RCL01 = 2nd Dsz 1006   R/S   015

     LRN

The Dsz statement is very useful in summing series. Consider

$$S = \sum_{i=1}^{\infty} \frac{1}{i^2 + 1} = \frac{1}{2} + \frac{1}{5} + \frac{1}{10} + \frac{1}{17} + \cdots. \tag{6}$$

Some preliminary transformations are necessary, since the convergence of the series is so slow that there is no practical way to evaluate it as it stands. After the first few terms, the general term is essentially $1/i^2$, and the error is of order $1/n$, where n is the number of terms considered. It would be necessary to consider several hundred terms to get even a reasonable estimate of the sum. The convergence can be greatly improved by using the known fact that

$$\sum_{i=1}^{\infty} \frac{1}{i^2} = \frac{\pi^2}{6}$$

* For an example of this, see the second program of chapter 3, section 6.
† The case n = 0 is considered further in section 5.

Then the desired result becomes

$$S = \frac{\pi^2}{6} - \sum_{i=1}^{\infty} \frac{1}{i^2(i^2+1)} \tag{7}$$

The general term is now essentially $1/i^4$, and the error is of order $1/n^3$. A further improvement is obtained by using the formula

$$\sum_{i=1}^{\infty} \frac{1}{i^4} = \frac{\pi^4}{90}$$

We now have

$$S = \pi^2 \left(\frac{1}{6} - \frac{\pi^2}{90} \right) + \sum_{i=1}^{\infty} \frac{1}{i^4(i^2+1)} \tag{8}$$

The general term is essentially $1/i^6$, and the error is of order $1/n^5$. The program follows

0	LRN	000
1	STO01 0 STO02	005
2	RCL01 x² + 1 = × RCL01 x² x² = $\frac{1}{x}$ SUM02	020
3	2nd Dsz 1005	024
4	6 $\frac{1}{x}$ − 2nd π x² ÷ 90 = × 2nd π x² + RCL02 = R/S	041
	LRN	

Contents of data registers

01 i = n − 1, ... , 1   02 partial sum

Press   n   RST   R/S

Display   S

The program is straightforward. Line 1 stores n in data register 01 and clears data register 02, which will contain the partial sum of the series. Lines 2 and 3 constitute a Dsz loop which evaluates each term in equation (8) and adds it to the partial sum in data register 02. The evaluation starts with the last term considered, $i = n$, and proceeds to the left as i is decreased by 1 in each succeeding cycle. Line 4 adds the first term on the right side of equation (8) to the sum of the series to obtain S, the value of the original series (6). The correct numerical result to ten significant figures is known to be 1.076674047. Results given by the program for several values of n are

n	5	10	20	40
S	1.076637	1.0766726	1.07667399	1.07667405

4. Unconditional transfers; subroutines

There are three unconditional transfer statements. We have already considered the RST (reset) statement; this transfers the execution of the program to location 000. Another unconditional transfer statement is GTO (go to), followed by a three digit program location number. This transfers the execution of the program to the location specified. The third unconditional transfer statement is the SBR (subroutine) statement, which is also followed by a three digit program location number which transfers the execution of the program to the location specified. The program runs until it reaches an INV SBR (inverse subroutine) statement, then returns to the original point. (These descriptions of the statements are not comprehensive; we emphasize only the points which will be used in this book. Complete discussions can be found in reference 1.)

It often happens that a function occurs repeatedly in an analysis. It is possible to punch the function into the calculator at each point in the program where it occurs, but a great deal of effort can be saved by using the SBR statement. To illustrate this, we consider the problem of evaluating

$$y = f(x_1) - 3f(x_2) + 2f(x_3) \tag{9}$$

where

$$f(x) = (3 - 5x + 2x^2 + x^3)^{1/2} \tag{10}$$

0	LRN			000
1	RCL01	SBR031	STO05	007
2	RCL02	SBR031 × 3 = INV SUM05		018
3	RCL03	SBR031 × 2 = SUM05	RCL05 R/S	031

4   STO04 + 2 = × RCL04 − 5 = × RCL04 + 3 = $\sqrt{x}$
    INV SBR   050

    LRN

Contents of data registers

01 x_1 02 x_2 03 x_3 04 x   05 partial sum

Input/output

Press x_1 STO01 x_2 STO02 x_3 STO03   RST   R/S

Display   y

The program is straightforward; the only thing new is the subroutine statement. The instruction SBR031 transfers the execution of the program to program location 031. The program then executes line 4, which is the subroutine. When it reaches the INV SBR statement it returns to the original point and continues with the main program. The subroutine of line 4 is adapted from the next to last program of section 1.

As a numerical example, we set $x_1 = 1$, $x_2 = 2$, $x_3 = 3$. The result is y = 3.48192 5293.

The use of a subroutine has another advantage in addition to making the program more concise. It often happens that one basic program is used many times for different functions—such as a program for numerical integration. By placing the function in a subroutine at the end, it is possible to leave the main program intact and rewrite only the subroutine each time the program is used. This is much more convenient than rewriting the entire program every time it is used.

Some caution must be exercised in using a subroutine. An equal sign in a subroutine completes all pending operations not only in the subroutine but also in the main program. One way to avoid trouble is to abandon the equal sign when writing subroutines and use parentheses instead. However, this leads to some rather clumsy and complicated subroutines. A better procedure is to avoid pending operations when using the subroutine statement in the main program. There is no difficulty in doing this; e.g. in line 2 we write

$$\text{SBR031} \times 3 \quad \textbf{not} \quad 3 \times \text{SBR031} \tag{11a,b}$$

It is important to see the difference between the two versions. In the first case the statements are written in the order in which they are executed: first the subroutine, then the multiplication. There is no pending operation. In the second case the multiplication *appears* first, but the subroutine is still *executed* first. The multiplication is pending while the subroutine is being executed, and it will be activated prematurely when the first equal sign is reached in the subroutine. To avoid this type of difficulty we shall use the form (11a) throughout this book.

5. Recurrence formulas; Legendre polynomials

Recurrence formulas occur in many practical problems, e.g. in the numerical solution of differential equations. The Exc (exchange) statement is very useful for problems of this type. Consider, for example

$$x_{i+1} = 3x_i - 2x_{i-1} + 1 \tag{12}$$

Two starting values x_1 and x_2 are specified, and it is required to find the subsequent values x_3, x_4, ... The program is

0	LRN					000
1	$3 \times$ RCL02 $- 2 \times$ RCL01 $+ 1 =$					012
2	2nd Exc 02	STO01	RCL02	R/S	RST	020
	LRN					

Input/output

Press x_1 STO01 x_2 STO02   RST   R/S   R/S   R/S

Display x_3 x_4 x_5

Line 1 is simply the equation. This is all that is necessary for one cycle. Line 2 shifts the contents of the data registers in preparation for the next cycle. The statement 2nd Exc 02 stores the new result x_3 in data register 02 and draws the previous content x_2 into the display register. This is then stored in data register 01, erasing x_1. x_3 is then recalled from data register 02, and this is displayed when the execution of the program ends with the R/S statement. The same description applies to subsequent cycles, except that the subscripts are increased by 1 for each repetition. The first cycle is put into action by pressing RST R/S. Subsequent cycles are activated by pressing R/S only, since an RST statement has been included at the end of line 2. As a numerical example, suppose that $x_1 = 1$ and $x_2 = 2$. Then we obtain the sequence 1, 2, 5, 12, 27, 58, 121, ... (It can be shown that the analytical solution is $x_i = 2^i - i$.)

The efficiency of the foregoing program can be enhanced by placing the exchange operation at the beginning instead of the end. Thus

0   LRN   000

1   2nd Exc 01 × 2 +/− + RCL01 × 3 + 1 = R/S
    RST   015

    LRN

Input/output

Press x_1 STO01 x_2 RST   R/S   R/S   R/S

Display x_3 x_4 x_5

Labels are sometimes used to simplify an input operation, at the cost of increased program length. The statements A through E and A′ through E′ are known as user-defined labels. When one of these keys is pressed in the input, the program starts running at the point where that parameter is labeled in the program. Rewriting the foregoing program with labels, we have

0	LRN	000
1	2nd Lbl A STO01 R/S	005
2	2nd Lbl B 2nd Exc 01 × 2 +/− + RCL01 × 3 + 1 = R/S	021
	LRN	

Input/output

Press x_1 A x_2 B   B   B

Display x_3 x_4 x_5

If we need only one specific result x_n instead of the entire sequence, it may be more convenient to use a Dsz loop. The program follows. The counter for the Dsz loop is stored in data register 00. The result x_n is obtained by running $n - 2$ cycles.

0	LRN	000
1	2nd Lbl A − 2 = STO00 R/S	008
2	2nd Lbl B STO01 R/S	013
3	2nd Lbl C 2nd Exc 01 × 2 +/− + RCL01 × 3 + 1 = 2nd Dsz 0015 R/S	033
	LRN	

Input/output

Press   n A x_1 B x_2 C

Display x_n

At this point it is desirable to introduce another new statement that will be needed for the next example. It is often necessary to add 1 to a counter in a data register. This can, of course, be done by using the SUM statement. For example, to add 1 to the number in data register 01, we can write 1 SUM01. Another way to accomplish this is provided by the statement 2nd Op 21. The statement 2nd Op followed by a 2 and one other digit adds 1 to the number in the single digit data register specified by the second digit. This procedure is a little more efficient than the SUM operation; it takes only two program steps instead of three. To subtract 1 we use the statement 2nd Op followed by a 3 and one other digit which specifies a single digit data register. This again takes only two program steps; otherwise we would have to write 1 INV SUM followed by the address of the data register, which takes four steps.

This method has another feature which is often more important than saving one or two program steps. It can be used at any time to adjust a counter in a data register without interrupting the calculation in progress. The number in the display register retains the value which it had before the incrementing procedure was used.

We now consider a problem which illustrates practically all of the points which have been considered thus far with the exception of the subroutine: a program to evaluate the Legendre polynomials. These are considered in advanced calculus. The first few are

$$P_0(x) = 1 \qquad P_1(x) = x \qquad P_2(x) = \frac{1}{2}(3x^2 - 1) \qquad (13a,b,c)$$

$$P_3(x) = \frac{x}{2}(5x^2 - 3) \qquad P_4(x) = \frac{1}{8}(35x^4 - 30x^2 + 3) \quad (13d,e)$$

$$P_5(x) = \frac{x}{8}(63x^4 - 70x^2 + 15) \qquad (13f)$$

It is possible to construct a program based upon the second order recurrence relation

$$P_{n+1}(x) = \frac{1}{n+1}[(2n+1) x P_n(x) - n P_{n-1}(x)] \qquad (14)$$

However, a much shorter and simpler program is obtained by using the two simultaneous first order recurrence relations (reference 6, page 99)

$$P'_n(x) = n\,P_{n-1}(x) + x\,P'_{n-1}(x) \qquad\qquad (15a)$$

$$P_n(x) = \frac{1}{n}[x\,P'_n(x) - P'_{n-1}(x)] \qquad\qquad (15b)$$

The primes denote differentiation with respect to x. The starting values are $P_0(x) = 1$ and $P'_0(x) = 0$. A program based upon equations (15) is preferable to one based upon (14) in two respects. It is shorter, and it evaluates $P'_n(x)$ as well as $P_n(x)$. Some applications require both parameters.

```
0   LRN                                                         000

1   2nd Lb1 A   STO01   R/S   2nd Lb1 B   STO02        009

2   0 STO03   x ⇌ t   RCL01   2nd x = t 052
    1 STO00                                                    021

3   × RCL00 + RCL02 × RCL03 = 2nd Exc 03           033

4   + / − + RCL02 × RCL03 = ÷ RCL00 =                 045

5   2nd Op 20   2nd Dsz 1021   R/S                         052

6   1 = R/S                                                     055

    LRN
```

Contents of data registers

00 n = 1, 2, 3, ...   01 n, n − 1, ... 1   02 x   03
$P'_{n-1}(x)$, $P'_n(x)$

Input/output

Press   n A   x B

Display $P_n(x)$

The program appears above. Line 1 labels and stores n and x. The parameter n in data register 01 will serve as the counter for a

Dsz loop. Line 2 stores 0 in data register 03. This is the appropriate value of $P'_{n-1}(x) = P'_0(x)$ for the first cycle. The data register 00 contains the value of n for each cycle, starting with 1. Line 2 also contains a conditional transfer for the case n = 0, which is considered in line 6. This is necessary because the Dsz loop of lines 3 to 5 breaks down when n = 0, as discussed in section 3. Line 3 represents equation (15a), and line 4 represents equation (15b). For the first cycle the number in the display register at the beginning of line 3 is $P_0(x) = 1$, which is the last entry of line 2. For each subsequent cycle the number in the display register at the beginning of line 3 is $P_{n-1}(x)$, which is the result $P_n(x)$ of the preceding cycle. The Exc03 statement at the end of line 3 replaces the old parameter $P'_{n-1}(x)$ in data register 03 with the new result $P'_n(x)$. The former parameter is brought into the display register for the beginning of line 4. When the RCL03 statement appears later in line 4, it is $P'_n(x)$ which is recalled. Line 5 uses the Op2- statement to increase the value of n in data register 00 by 1 for each cycle, and also executes the Dsz loop and displays the final result, $P_n(x)$. If the value of $P'_n(x)$ is required, it is obtained by pressing RCL03.

A slightly more compact program is obtained below by handling the case n = 0 in a different way. Instead of placing a Dsz statement at the end of the cycle, we place an INV Dsz (decrement and skip on nonzero) statement at the beginning. Now the decrementing takes place before the cycle is run instead of after. The initial value of the counter must be greater by 1 than the desired number of cycles. To take care of this, the Op 21 statement is used in line 2.

0	LRN	000
1	2nd Lbl A STO01 R/S 2nd Lb1 B STO02	009
2	0 STO03 1 STO00 2nd Op 21	017
3	INV 2nd Dsz 1051	022
4	× RCL00 + RCL02 × RCL03 = 2nd Exc 03	034
5	+/− + RCL02 × RCL03 = ÷ RCL00=	046
6	2nd Op 20 GTO017 R/S	052
	LRN	

Contents of data registers

00 1, 2, 3, ... 01 n, n $+$ 1, n, n $-$ 1, ... 1 02 x
03 $P'_{n-1}(x)$, $P'_n(x)$

Input/output

Press n A x B

Display $P_n(x)$

In both of the examples of this section, the parameters have only a single index (subscript). In a problem of this type, the results of successive cycles form a one-dimensional array. There are more complicated recurrence formulas involving parameters with double subscripts. Results for a problem of this type form a two-dimensional array. The procedure is more complicated than the one used here. The Exc statement is used in conjunction with indirect addressing. An example of this type appears later in chapter 4, section 3.

Some further remarks about labels may be of interest. Labels can be used for addressing instead of program location numbers: such as GTO A, SBR A. Labels are used very extensively in reference 1. However, this increases the running time of a program. Each time that a label is addressed, the calculator must search for its location. The search begins at program location 000 and progresses through program memory until the desired location is found. In this book labels are used only where they serve to simplify the input/output operation.

6. Indirect addressing; Lagrange interpolation

It sometimes happens that a calculation is well suited to the use of a Dsz loop except that the expression contains some coefficient which cannot be obtained from any simple equation, and must be found from a table for each cycle. One solution to this problem is to abandon the Dsz loop and write out the program directly for the entire calculation. However, it is often more convenient to use the Dsz loop and punch the tabular values into the input, then transfer them into the program by indirect addressing. To illustrate the technique, we shall write a program for the sum of the series

$$\cot x = \frac{1}{x} - \frac{x}{3} - \frac{x^3}{45} - \frac{2x^5}{945} - \frac{x^7}{4725} - \frac{2x^9}{93555} - \cdots \quad (16)$$

The program is

```
0   LRN                                              000

1   STO10  1/x  STO11  5 STO00                       008

2   RCL10 yˣ (2 × RCL00 − 1) = ÷ RCL 2nd Ind00
    = INV SUM 11                                      027

3   2nd Dsz 0008   RCL11   R/S                        034

    LRN
```

Contents of data registers

00 5,4,3,2,1   01 3   02 45   03 472.5   04 4725
05 46777.5   10 x   11 partial sum

Input/output

Press   3 STO01   45 STO02   472.5 STO03   4725 STO04
        46777.5 STO05   x   RST   R/S

Display   cot x

The negative reciprocals of the coefficients (starting with the $-x/3$ term) are stored in data registers 01 through 05. Line 1 stores x in data register 10. (The number 10 is chosen arbitrarily in order to leave enough space for the coefficients of any number of terms of the series likely to be used.) Line 1 also stores the first term $1/x$ in data register 11, and stores the number 5 in data register 00. This is used as the counter for the Dsz loop. Line 2 calculates the general term and adds it to the partial sum in data register 11. The statement RCL 2nd Ind 00 recalls the number that is stored in the data register whose address is found in data register 00. Line 3 executes the Dsz loop and recalls and displays the result. The calculation starts with the last term and proceeds from right to left.

This program has little or no practical value; it is given here to illustrate the use of indirect addressing. The easiest way to evaluate cot x is to press 2ndRad 2ndtan 1/x.

At times it is necessary to obtain a value of a function from a table by interpolation. With a good table it is usually possible to obtain satisfactory accuracy for most engineering calculations by linear interpolation. This can easily be done manually on the calculator, and a program is not necessary. However, if high accuracy is required or if the available table gives results only for widely spaced values of the argument, higher order interpolation is needed unless the argument coincides with one of the tabulated values. One commonly used procedure is known as Lagrange interpolation, in which the desired function is approximated by a polynomial of order n − 1, using data from n points. For a cubic polynomial, the formula is

$$y = \frac{(x - x_2)(x - x_3)(x - x_4)}{(x_1 - x_2)(x_1 - x_3)(x_1 - x_4)}\, y_1 + \frac{(x - x_3)(x - x_4)(x - x_1)}{(x_2 - x_3)(x_2 - x_4)(x_2 - x_1)}\, y_2$$
$$+ \frac{(x - x_4)(x - x_1)(x - x_2)}{(x_3 - x_4)(x_3 - x_1)(x_3 - x_2)}\, y_3 + \frac{(x - x_1)(x - x_2)(x - x_3)}{(x_4 - x_1)(x_4 - x_2)(x_4 - x_3)}\, y_4 \qquad (17)$$

It is clear that this equation is exact at the four base points. The base points do not have to be uniformly spaced, although they usually are when the method is used to interpolate in values from a table. Two base points are chosen below and two above the value of x for which y is to be evaluated. The program follows:

0	LRN	000
1	4 ST009 0 ST019	006
2	3 ST000	009
3	RCL10 − RCL 2nd Ind 00 = ÷ (RCL04 − RCL 2nd Ind 00) =	024
4	2nd Prd 14 2nd Dsz 0009 RCL14 SUM19	034

5 RCL01   2nd Exc 02   2nd Exc 03   2nd Exc 04
   STO01   044

6 RCL11   2nd Exc 12   2nd Exc 13   STO14   052

7 2nd Dsz 9006   RCL19   R/S   059
   LRN

Contents of data registers

00 m   01 x_1 02 x_2 03 x_3 04 x_4 09 n

10 x   11 y_1 12 y_2 13 y_3 14 y_4 19 partial sum

Input/output

Press x_1 STO01 x_2 STO02 x_3 STO03 x_4 STO04
        x STO10 y_1 STO11 y_2 STO12 y_3 STO13
        y_4 STO14 R/S

Display   y

The program consists of two Dsz loops. Line 1 stores the number
n = 4 in data register 09. This is the counter for the outer Dsz loop,
which runs from line 2 to line 7. This loop evaluates and sums the
four terms on the right side of equation (17). Line 1 also clears data
register 19, which will contain the partial sums as the terms are found.
Line 2 stores the number m = 3 in data register 00. This is the counter
for the inner Dsz loop, which appears in lines 3 and 4. Line 3 calculates
$(x - x_3)/(x_4 - x_3)$ on the first cycle, $(x - x_2)/(x_4 - x_2)$ on the second
cycle, and $(x - x_1)/(x_4 - x_1)$ on the third cycle. (The appropriate
data registers are found by using the indirect recall statement.) Line
4 multiplies y_4 by these results to obtain the fourth term on the right
side of equation (17) and adds this result to the content of data register
19. Lines 5 and 6 shift the x_i's and y_i's to the next higher data registers,
and line 7 executes the outer Dsz loop. The second time the cycle is
run it calculates the third term on the right side of equation (17);
the third and fourth times it calculates the second and first terms.
The final sum is then recalled in line 7. The data registers 05 through
08 and 15 through 18 are left vacant so the program can easily be
expanded to handle data from 6 points or 8 points. The contents of

the data registers are shown as they stand at the beginning of the program: for example n, not n, n − 1, ... 1.

A further comment about lines 5 and 6 may be desirable. The exchange operations for the x_i's and the y_i's are not identical. Each x_i is used several times in the evaluation of the terms on the right side of equation (17). Therefore the x_i's are fully recycled in line 5; the value which has reached station 4 is moved to station 1. No values are lost; all of the x_i's can be recovered after the program is run by pressing RCL01, RCL02, ... On the other hand, each y_i is used only once, so it is not necessary to store the values after they reach station 4.

To illustrate the use of the program we calculate the Bessel function $J_0(x)$ for $x = 1.15$. The following values are found on page 390 of reference 3:

i	1	2	3	4
x_i	1.0	1.1	1.2	1.3
$J_0(x_i)$	.7651977	.7196320	.6711327	.6200860

The program gives the result $x = .6957249$; the correct value is .6957198. The calculated result is correct to five significant figures.

It is sometimes necessary to use inverse interpolation, that is to find the value of an independent variable corresponding to some specified value of the dependent variable. Lagrange interpolation is well suited to this problem, since the base points do not have to be equally spaced. We use exactly the same procedure as that just given, but call the dependent variable x and the independent variable y.

The practical utility of higher order interpolation is rather limited. Results can usually be obtained with better accuracy and less labor by evaluating the function directly. Programs for Legendre polynomials have been given in section 5; programs for a number of other higher mathematical functions are given in chapter 3. If you want to use a table, the best procedure is to find a good table with reasonably closely spaced values of the argument. Most of the tables of reference 3 give results only for very widely spaced values of the argument. They are very good for checking a program or for examples in which the argument can be chosen to fit the table, but they are not suitable for practical problems.

A program for sorting numbers provides an excellent illustration of indirect addressing. Suppose that we have a sequence of numbers arranged in random order. We want to write a program to arrange them in correct numerical order, increasing from left to right. Before writing the program, it may be helpful to consider how the sorting process will be organized. We need two Dsz loops. The inner loop compares successive pairs of data and arranges each pair in correct order, running from left to right through the sequence. The outer loop then repeats this operation. If there are n input numbers, the inner loop initially runs n − 1 times; the outer loop also runs n − 1 times. We trace the following input data through n − 1 = 4 cycles of the inner loop (1 cycle of the outer loop):

```
5   4   3   2   1
4   5   3   2   1
4   3   5   2   1
4   3   2   5   1
4   3   2   1   5
```

The highest number is now at the right. For the next cycle of the outer loop, we need only n − 2 = 3 cycles of the inner loop. The result is

```
3   2   1   4   5
```

The third and fourth cycles of the outer loop lead to

```
2   1   3   4   5
1   2   3   4   5
```

which is the desired result. The required number of cycles of the inner loop decreases by 1 with each successive cycle of the outer loop.

0	LRN	000
1	2nd Lbl A 2 STO00 1 +/− STO02 R/S	010
2	2nd Lbl B 2nd Op 20 STO 2nd Ind 00 2nd Op 22 R/S	019
3	2nd Lbl C 2 STO00 RCL02 STO01	028
4	2nd Op 20 RCL 2nd Ind 00 x ⇌ t 2nd Op 20 RCL 2nd Ind 00 2nd x ≥ t 044	040

5	x ⇌ t 2nd Exc 2nd Ind 00 x ⇌ t	044
6	x ⇌ t 2nd Op 30 STO 2nd Ind 00	049
7	2nd Dsz 1028	053
8	2nd Dsz 2021	057
9	2nd Lbl D RCL 2nd Ind 00 2nd Op 20 R/S	064

LRN

The program appears above. Line 1 stores the appropriate starting values of an index for indirect addressing in data register 00 and the counter for the outer Dsz loop in data register 02. Data register 01 will contain the counter for the inner Dsz loop; subsequent data registers starting with 03 will contain the input numbers, which are inserted in line 2. Line 3 is the first line of the outer Dsz loop, which runs to line 8. It stores the starting values for the inner Dsz loop, which runs from line 4 through 7. Line 4 compares two successive numbers to see whether they are in the correct order (with the larger number at the right). If they are not, line 5 interchanges them. If they are, line 5 is skipped. Line 6 transfers the smaller number from the test register to the appropriate data register. Line 7 completes the inner Dsz loop. Line 8 completes the outer Dsz loop. Line 9 delivers the output.

The input/output operation for the sequence given above is

Press   A   5 B   4 B   3 B   2 B   1 B   C   D   D   D   D

Display   1   2   3   4   5

The basic program can handle 27 numbers on the TI-58 or 57 numbers on the TI-59. This capacity can be expanded to 47 numbers on the TI-58 or 97 numbers on the TI-59 by repartitioning the memory before inserting the program. The procedure is discussed in the next section. However, the running time is undesirably long for very long sequences.

7. Further topics

Accuracy of input/output data. The calculator display shows 10 significant figures, but the calculations are made with 13 significant figures to guard against roundoff errors. Ten significant figure accuracy is

28

far more than necessary for most scientific and engineering calculations. However, it is possible to extract a full 13 digit result if desired. We shall do this for $\sqrt{3}$. We perform the following keyboard operations

Press   3 $\sqrt{x}$ $\times$ 100 $-$ 173 $=$

Display   .2050807568

It follows that

$$\sqrt{3} = .01(173 + .2050807568) = 1.732050807568$$

This type of procedure is almost never necessary. Also, it is often inapplicable. It succeeds after a one step calculation like the one just considered, but does not work after a lengthy calculation because the last few digits are usually lost to roundoff errors.

The inverse problem is more important. The calculator accepts input data only to 10 significant figures. However, in order to make the provision against roundoff error effective, it is sometimes necessary to insert data to the full 13 digit capacity of the calculator. To do this it is necessary to break a number into two parts and insert each part separately. We will show the procedure for Euler's constant γ. To thirteen significant figures, this is $\gamma = .57721\ 56649\ 015$. We store this number in data register 01 by the following steps:

$$577 + .21566\ 49015 = \div 1000 = STO01$$

This operation can be verified by using the method of the preceding paragraph to recover the full 13 digit number.

Editing programs. It is very easy to make a mistake in punching a program into the calculator. It is often possible to catch a mistake immediately after it is made. Suppose that an operator suspects that he has accidentally hit the wrong key on the last step. This can be checked by referring to the two-digit number in the display register, which is the key code number of the next program step. As long as the program is being punched in normally in the forward direction, this number is 00. The last step is checked by pressing the BST (back step) key.* A nonzero two-digit number will then appear in the display. This is the key code number of the last step. A table on page V-50 of the manual (reference 1) gives the statement corresponding to each

---

* There are four editing keys: SST, BST, Ins and Del. These are discussed thoroughly on page IV-21 of the manual (reference 1).

key code number. If the statement is wrong, it is corrected by simply punching in the correct statement, overwriting the incorrect one. If it is correct, the current program location may be reached by pressing the SST (single step) key.

Routine checks should be made while punching in a program, even if no error is suspected. The three-digit number which appears in the display when the calculator is in the learn mode is the program location number. After punching in each line, this number should be checked against the number at the right of the line in the printed program. If it is less than the printed number, a step has been missed. If it is greater than the printed number, an extra step has been punched in. Usually the most convenient way to find the error is to return to the beginning of the line, i.e., to the program location shown at the right of the preceding line in the printed program. This is accomplished by pressing the BST key repeatedly. An alternate method is to press LRN, returning the calculator to keyboard operation, then press GTO followed by the desired program location number, then again press LRN. The next step is to identify the first statement which has been punched into the line. We do this by referring to the key code number in the display register, again using the table on page V-50 of the manual. This statement should agree with the corresponding one in the printed program. We proceed step by step through the line by using the SST key, checking each statement against the corresponding one in the printed program. If there is a missing step, it can be inserted by using the Ins (insert) key. An alternate procedure is to punch in the correct steps from the point where the error is found to the end of the line, overwriting the previous statements. If there is an extra step, it is deleted by using the Del (delete) key. After the faulty line has been corrected, the remainder of the program is punched into the calculator in the ordinary way.

The foregoing procedures do not necessarily eliminate all errors; it is still possible that a wrong key may have been pressed without the operator being aware of it and without affecting the total number of steps. The best way to check a program is to run a test case with known results immediately after punching in the program and before applying it to a new problem. If this is tried and the program fails, a more thorough check is necessary. This is accomplished by pressing RST with the calculator still in the keyboard mode, then pressing LRN. The entire program is then checked step by step against the printed program by using the SST key and the table on page V-50 of the manual. This procedure is not as tedious as it might appear; after a little practice, it is easy to remember the code numbers of the most commonly used statements, so it is not necessary to refer to the table at every step.

Repartitioning the memory. In normal operation the TI-58 memory contains 30 data registers and 240 program steps. The TI-59 memory contains 60 data registers and 480 program steps. It is possible to trade data storage space for program memory space; a block of 10 data registers corresponds to 80 program steps. This is accomplished by pressing a number 0–10, say n, which represents a block of 10n data registers, followed by 2nd Op 17. For example, the instruction 2 2nd Op 17 results in a capacity of 20 data registers. On the TI-58, this leaves 320 program steps; on the TI-59, it leaves 800 program steps.

Manuals and program libraries. Two manuals (references 1 and 2) and a program library module are supplied with the calculator. No attempt is made to duplicate all of this material in the present book. Only the statements and techniques that are needed for our purposes are considered in detail. There are a number of keys which are never used in this book. Most users never need all of the capabilities of the calculator; some statements and techniques are very useful in certain specialized applications but seldom useful in other fields. An example of this is the material on statistical analysis in reference 1, pages V-32–40. This can be very useful in the analysis of experimental data and in some other applications. Also, there is a strong element of personal choice in the construction of a program. For a given problem, two programmers may write programs which look radically different and even use different keys, but accomplish the same thing. There are several differences in viewpoint between reference 1 and this book. (Compare, for example, the last paragraph of section 4 with the discussion at the bottom of page IV-49 and the top of page IV-51 of reference 1. Also see problem 3.) The best advice for the reader is to skim through reference 1 completely and study whatever points appear to be useful for his needs.

A collection of programs known as the Master Library is supplied with the TI-58/59 Calculator. Other libraries can be purchased separately. A program library consists of a program module and an instruction manual. The Master Library module is in the calculator as purchased; this can be removed and replaced by other modules for special applications. The corresponding manual is reference 2. Discussions of program libraries can be found in reference 1, section III, and reference 2, pages 1–5. You are advised to look through the list of programs in reference 2. Most of these are not duplicated in this book. Programs ML-02 and ML-03 for matrices and simultaneous equations are particularly important.

To illustrate a very simple application of a library program, we shall calculate the complex number $(2 + i)^2$ by using program ML-

05, following the directions on page 20 of reference 2. We turn the calculator on and perform the following operations:

Press   2nd Prg 05   2 A   1 A   C   x ⇌ t

Display   3   4

The result is $3 + 4i$, which can easily be verified directly.

It is sometimes possible to use a library program as an adjunct to a prepared program. Then the library program serves the same purpose as a subroutine. There is an advantage, however, in using a library program instead of an ordinary subroutine—a library program does not take up space in the calculator program memory. In this manner the effective capacity of the calculator is increased. This use of library programs is discussed in reference 1, pages IV-52 and V-60–62. It is essential that the data registers used in the main program be consistent with those used in the library program.

As an example, we shall write a program to evaluate

$$w = 2z^2 - 3z + 4$$

where $z = x + iy$ and $w = u + iv$ are complex numbers. We shall use program ML-05 to evaluate z^2. Before writing the program we refer to page 21 of reference 2 to find what data registers are used in the library program. We find that data registers 01 and 02 are used to store x and y, respectively. We use these data registers in the same way in the main program. Data registers 03 and 04 are also used in the library program, apparently to store some intermediate results which are not specified. We skip these data registers in the main program. The program follows:

0	LRN		000
1	2nd Lbl A STO01 R/S		005
2	2nd Lbl B STO02		009
3	4 − 3 × RCL01 = STO05		018
4	3 × RCL02 = +/− STO06		026
5	2nd Prg 05 C × 2 = SUM05 x ⇌ t × 2 =		
	SUM06		040

6 RCL05 R/S RCL06 R/S 046

LRN

Contents of data registers

01 x 02 y 03 used 04 used 05 u 06 v

Input/output

Press x A y B R/S

Display   u   v

Lines 1 and 2 assign the labels A and B to x and y, respectively. Line 3 calculates the real part of $4 - 3z$ and stores it in data register 05. Line 4 calculates the imaginary part and stores it in data register 06. Line 5 calls the library program ML-05 and uses it to calculate the real and imaginary parts of $2z^2$. These are added to the contents of data registers 05 and 06, which now contain u and v, respectively. Line 6 recalls and displays u. The value of v is displayed by pressing R/S. As a numerical example, let $z = 2 + i$. Then the program gives the result $w = 4 + 5i$, which can easily be verified directly.

In the foregoing examples the library program is treated essentially as a "black box"; we are not concerned with the internal structure of the library program. This is by far the most common way in which library programs are used. However, if for some reason it is necessary to analyze a library program, this is easily accomplished by bringing it into the calculator program memory (reference 1, page III-4) and then using the editing procedures discussed earlier in this section.

Problems

1. Write programs to evaluate the following functions:
   (a) $y = 5 - 3x + 2x^2 + 3x^3 - x^4$
   (b) $y = 2x^5 - x^4 + 3x^3 + 2x^2 - x - 1$
   (c) $y = e^{3x} - x^2 + 5x^3 - \cos x$
   (d) $y = x^3 \ln x + x^2 - 3x + 2 \sin x$
   (e) $y = e^x \cos x + e^{-x} \sin x$
   Check the programs by obtaining numerical results with $x = 2$.

Ans. (a) 15 (b) 77 (c) 439.84494 (d) 4.4544749 (e) −2.9518723

2. Write programs for the following functions:
   (a) $y = 2x - 3$, $x \leq -1$; $y = x^2 + 6x$, $x \geq -1$
   (b) $y = (x - 2)^2$, $x \leq 2$; $y = 0$, $x \geq 2$
   (c) $y = e^x$, $x \leq 2$; $y = 1$, $x > 2$

3. A bank has the following service charges for checks:
   $0.10 per check for the first five checks (1–5)

   .09 per check for the next five (6–10)

   .08 per check for the next five (11–15)

   .07 per check for each check over 15

   Write a program to calculate the total service charge. (This problem is taken from reference 1, pp. IV-93–98. One program is given there; another can be found at the back of this book.)

4. Write programs to evaluate the following finite sums. (The analytical expressions for the sums are given to make it easy to check the programs.)

   (a) $1^2 + 2^2 + 3^2 + \ldots + n^2 = \dfrac{n}{6}(n + 1)(2n + 1)$

   (b) $1^2 + 3^2 + 5^2 + \ldots + (2n - 1)^2 = \dfrac{n}{3}(4n^2 - 1)$

   (c) $1^3 + 2^3 + 3^3 + \ldots + n^3 = \left[\dfrac{n}{2}(n + 1)\right]^2$

   (d) $1^3 + 3^3 + 5^3 + \cdots + (2n - 1)^3 = n^2(2n^2 - 1)$

5. Write programs to evaluate the following infinite series. (The analytical expressions for the sums are given to make it easy to check the programs.)

   (a) $\left(\dfrac{1}{1 \cdot 2 \cdot 3}\right)^2 + \left(\dfrac{1}{2 \cdot 3 \cdot 4}\right)^2 + \left(\dfrac{1}{3 \cdot 4 \cdot 5}\right)^2$

   $$+ \ldots = \dfrac{\pi^2}{4} - \dfrac{39}{16}$$

   (b) $\dfrac{1}{1 \cdot 2 \cdot 3} + \dfrac{1}{5 \cdot 6 \cdot 7} + \dfrac{1}{9 \cdot 10 \cdot 11} + \ldots = \dfrac{1}{4}\ln 2$

   (c) $1 - \dfrac{1}{2 \cdot 2} + \dfrac{1}{3 \cdot 2^2} - \dfrac{1}{4 \cdot 2^3} + \ldots = 2\ln\dfrac{3}{2}$

   (d) $1 - \dfrac{1}{3 \cdot 3} + \dfrac{1}{5 \cdot 3^2} - \dfrac{1}{7 \cdot 3^3} + \ldots = \dfrac{\pi}{2\sqrt{3}}$

(e) $1 - \dfrac{1}{3} + \dfrac{1 \cdot 2}{3 \cdot 5} - \dfrac{1 \cdot 2 \cdot 3}{3 \cdot 5 \cdot 7} + \ldots = \dfrac{2}{\sqrt{3}} \ln \dfrac{\sqrt{3}+1}{\sqrt{2}}$

6. Write programs for the following recurrence formulas and use them to find the first few values of y_i.

(a) $y_{i+1} - 5y_i + 6y_{i-1} = 0 \qquad y_1 = 1, \; y_2 = 2$
Ans. $y_i = 1, 2, 4, 8, 16, 32, \ldots$.

(b) $y_{i+1} - 2y_i + 2y_{i-1} = 0 \qquad y_1 = 3, \; y_2 = 5$
Ans. $y_i = 3, 5, 4, -2, -12, -20, \ldots$.

7. Show that the integral

$$I_n = \int_0^{\pi/2} x^n \sin dx \qquad n = 0,1,2, \ldots$$

satisfies the recurrence formula

$$I_{n+1} = (n+1)\left[\left(\frac{\pi}{2}\right)^n - n I_{n-1}\right]$$

Also show by elementary integration that $I_0 = I_1 = 1$. Write a program to evaluate $I_2, I_3, \ldots$.

Ans. 1.1415927, 1.4022033, 1.8040265, 2.3962749

8. An operator wishes to calculate the value of I_{10} in problem 7. He starts to run the sequence $I_2, I_3, \ldots$ but loses his place and forgets what value of n corresponds to the current value of I_n in the display register. How can he find the correct value of n without recalculating the entire sequence?

9. Find the terms x_{20} and x_{21} of the sequence of section 5 for equation (12).
Ans. $x_{20} = 1048556 \quad x_{21} = 2097131$

10. The Hermite polynomials are considered in advanced calculus. The first few are

$H_0(x) = 1 \qquad H_1(x) = 2x \qquad H_3(x) = 4x^2 - 2$
$H_3(x) = 3x^3 - 12x \qquad H_4(x) = 16x^4 - 48x^2 + 12$

By using the recurrence formulas

$$H'_n(x) = 2n H_{n-1}(x) \qquad H_n(x) = \frac{x}{n} H'_n(x) - H'_{n-1}(x)$$

or otherwise, write a program to evaluate the Hermite polynomials. Numerical results to check the program for values of n from 0 through 4 can easily be obtained from the basic formulas above.

11. Write a program to evaluate the binomial coefficient

$$\binom{p}{q} = \frac{p!}{q!(p-q)!}$$

Numerical results to check the program can be found in almost any mathematics handbook.

12. Revise the program of section 6 for Lagrange interpolation to utilize data from six base points. Given the values $J_0(.9) = .80752\ 37981$ and $J_0(1.4) = .5685\ 51204$, obtain a more accurate value of $J_0(1.15)$ than the one found in the text.

2

ROOTS
OF EQUATIONS

1. The method of iteration

It is often necessary to find the roots of various types of equations. In this chapter we shall consider several methods of solving equations. We start with the method of iteration. To solve the equation

$$y = f(x) = 0 \qquad (1)$$

We write it in the form

$$x = \phi(x) \qquad (2)$$

It is often possible to solve the equation very easily by first obtaining a preliminary estimate of x from a rough plot of the function, then substituting this into the right side of equation (2). If the procedure is successful, the resulting value on the left will be closer to the true value than the original estimate. This procedure is repeated as many times as necessary until the desired accuracy is obtained.

Consider the equation

$$y = x^2 - 2x - 4 = 0 \qquad (3)$$

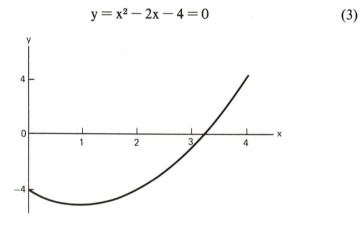

FIGURE 1

which is sketched in the above. We write

$$x = (4 + 2x)^{1/2} \qquad (4)$$

The iteration program is simply

0	LRN	000
1	×2+4=$\sqrt{x}$ R/S RST	008
	LRN	

38

From the sketch of Fig. 1, we obtain x = 3.2 for a rough estimate of the root. To run the program we press 3.2 RST R/S. The displayed result is then used as the starting value for the next cycle. Subsequent results are obtained by pressing R/S; the RST statement at the end of line 1 resets the program pointer automatically in preparation for the next cycle. Thus we obtain the sequence

3.2	3.225	3.2326	3.2350	3.23574	3.23597
3.23604	3.236058	3.236065	3.2360670		
3.2360677	3.2360679				

As a second example, consider the equation

$$y = x - \frac{1}{2}\ln x - 3 = 0 \tag{5}$$

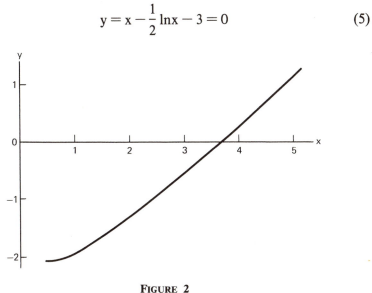

FIGURE 2

which is sketched in the above. We write

$$x = \frac{1}{2}\ln x + 3 \tag{6}$$

The iteration program is

0	LRN	000
1	ln x ÷ 2 + 3 = R/S RST	008
	LRN	

From the sketch of Fig. 2, we obtain x = 3.6 for a rough estimate of the root. The operation of the program is the same as in the preceding example. We press 3.6 RST R/S for the first result and R/S for each subsequent result. Thus we obtain the sequence

3.6   3.640   3.6461   3.6468   3.64693
3.646943   3.6469446   3.64694486   3.64694490

As a third example, consider the equation

$$y = \tan x - x = 0 \tag{7}$$

which is sketched in Fig. 3. We write

$$x = \text{arc tan } x \tag{8}$$

In the present example it is essential to look at Fig. 3 before writing the program. The desired root is approximately 4.4, which is in the third quadrant. Since the inverse trigonometric functions given by the calculator are principal values, it is necessary to increase the arc tangent by π. The program is

0   LRN   000

1   2nd Rad   INV 2nd tan + 2nd π = R/S   RST   008

LRN

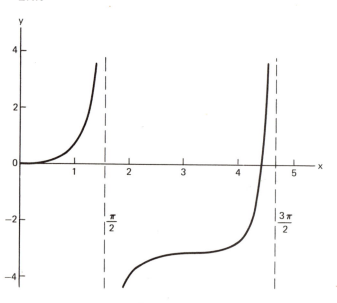

FIGURE 3

The operation of the program is the same as in the preceding two examples. We press 4.4 RST R/S for the first result and R/S for each subsequent result. Thus we obtain the sequence

4.4	4.489	4.4932	4.49340	4.493409
4.49340944	4.493409457	4.493409458		

It is obvious that, given an equation $y = f(x) = 0$, the choice of the equation $x = \phi(x)$ is essentially arbitrary. For example, given equation (7), we could have chosen to write $x = \tan x$ instead of equation (8). This choice has a very strong effect upon the convergence of the iteration process. In fact, an iterative evaluation of the equation $x = \tan x$ diverges. The iterative process is depicted graphically in Fig. 4. We start by assuming a value x_0. The function $\phi(x_0)$ which is the ordinate at point P then becomes the starting value x_1 for the next cycle. The new abscissa x_1 is located by drawing the horizontal and vertical lines shown. If the evaluation is successful, the process converges toward the exact result at point Q. Convergence occurs provided that the slope $d\phi/dx$ satisfies the inequality $|d\phi/dx| < 1$. It works best if the curve $y = \phi(x)$ is approximately horizontal, i.e., if $d\phi/dx$ is close to zero. This fact is often helpful in choosing a suitable form of the iterative equation.

To illustrate these remarks, we return to equation (5). It can be seen that the iteration based upon equation (6) succeeded because

$$\frac{d\phi}{dx} = \frac{1}{2x} \approx \frac{1}{2 \cdot 3.6} \approx .14$$

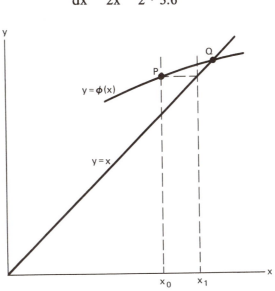

FIGURE 4

which is inside the interval of convergence. An extension of the plot of Fig. 2 shows that there is a second root $x \approx .0025$. If equation (6) is used to evaluate this root by iteration, we have $d\phi/dx \approx 200$, so the process may be expected to diverge. This turns out to be true; we obtain the sequence

$$.0025 \qquad .0043 \qquad .272 \qquad 2.35$$

We now try a different iterative equation, that is

$$x = e^{2x-6}$$

Then

$$\frac{d\phi}{dx} = 2e^{2x-6} = 2x \approx .005$$

and the process may be expected to converge. The program is

```
0   LRN                                              000

1   x 2 − 6 = INV ln x   R/S   RST                   009

    LRN
```

We obtain the sequence

$$.0025 \qquad .0024912 \qquad .002491133 \qquad .0024911328$$

The convergence of the iteration process is affected by the choice of the starting value, but it is difficult to predict this effect in advance. We now return to equation (8) and start the evaluation with a very poor guess, say $x = 4.0$. The next value will be 4.467, which is somewhat better than the starting value 4.4 which we actually used. Hence the worst that can happen is that the poor initial guess will necessitate one extra cycle in the iterative process. In some other problems the effect of a poor initial guess is greater, but in general the simple iteration process is somewhat less sensitive to the initial guess than some other methods are.

The problem of finding a root of an equation is often part of some larger problem. Suppose, for example, that we want to evaluate

$$z = \frac{x^2 - 16}{2} \tag{9}$$

where x is given by equation (7). One way to do this is to use the following program:

```
0   LRN                                                          000

1   2nd Rad   RCL01   INV 2nd tan + 2nd π   =
    STO01                                                        010

2   x² − 16 = ÷ 2 = R/S   RST                                    020

    LRN
```

Line 1 represents equation (8) and line 2 represents equation (9). It is necessary to store x. To run the program we press 4.4 STO01 RST R/S. Subsequent results are obtained by pressing R/S. Thus we obtain the sequence

2.075   2.0944   2.09532   2.095362   2.0953642
2.09536427

It is sometimes possible to obtain a shorter program by first putting the algebraic equation into optimum form. We can save two steps in the present program by rewriting equation (9) as $y = x^2/2 − 8$. Then the program becomes

```
0   LRN                                                          000

1   2nd Rad   RCL01   INV 2nd tan + 2nd π =
    STO01                                                        010

2   x² ÷ 2 − 8 = R/S   RST                                       018

    LRN
```

In later programs, transformations of this type will sometimes be used without comment.

In more complicated problems it is inefficient to run the entire program each time. It is preferable to iterate only the root finder segment, then complete the calculation after the root has been found to the desired degree of accuracy. We therefore rewrite the program as follows:

```
0   LRN                                                          000

1   2nd Rad   INV 2nd tan + 2nd π = R/S   RST                    008
```

$$2 \quad x^2 \div 2 - 8 = R/S \qquad\qquad\qquad\qquad \text{015}$$

LRN

We again press 4.4 STO01 RST R/S for the first result and R/S for each subsequent value of x. We obtain the same sequence which was found for equation (8). The final result is then found by pressing GTO008 R/S. This is 2.09536 428.

2. The Newton-Raphson method

The Newton-Raphson method is also an iterative method of solving an equation of the type $y = f(x) = 0$. However, instead of choosing the equation $x = \phi(x)$ arbitrarily, we adopt a more systematic viewpoint. Consider the Taylor series

$$y = y_0 + (x - x_0)y_0' + \frac{1}{2}(x - x_0)^2 y_0'' + \ldots.$$

By taking only two terms on the right and solving for x, we obtain the equation

$$x = x_0 + \frac{y - y_0}{y_0}$$

For the desired result $y = 0$, this becomes

$$x = x_0 - \frac{y_0}{y_0'} \qquad\qquad\qquad (10)$$

We now apply the method to equation (3). Let

$$y = x^2 - 2x - 4 = 0$$

then

$$y' = 2x - 2$$

It follows that

$$x = x_0 - \frac{x_0^2 - 2x_0 - 4}{2x_0 - 2} = \frac{x_0^2 + 4}{2(x_0 - 1)} \qquad\qquad (11)$$

44

Equation (11) is a little more complicated than the analogous equation (4) that we used in solving the problem by the simple iteration method. We now have to store the value of x. The program is

0   LRN   000

1   ST001 $x^2 + 4 = \div\ 2 \div (RCL01 - 1) = R/S$ RST   018

    LRN

Input/output

Press x_0 RST   R/S   R/S   R/S

Display x_1 x_2 x_3

As in section 1, we start with the estimate $x_0 = 3.2$. Then we obtain the sequence

3.2   3.2364   3.236068   3.23606798

In this example the Newton-Raphson method is much more efficient than the simple iteration method.

The most straightforward method of setting up a program is not always the most efficient. It is sometimes possible to obtain a neater and more compact program by a trick. We shall do this for the foregoing example. We rewrite equation (11) as

$$x = \frac{1}{2}\left(x_0 - 1 + \frac{5}{x_0 - 1} + 2\right) \tag{12}$$

The program now becomes

0   LRN   000

1   $-1 = + \dfrac{1}{x} \times 5 + 2 = \div\ 2 = R/S$ RST   015

    LRN

This time nothing is stored. The new program is slightly shorter than the original one. The input/output operation is not changed. We again start with the estimate $x_0 = 3.2$. The results are identical to those found with the first program.

In this problem it is questionable whether there is any advantage in using the more sophisticated method. The second program is slightly faster than the first, but some preliminary work is required to arrive at equation (12).

We again consider equation (5), which is

$$y = x - \frac{1}{2} \ln x - 3 = 0$$

It is clear that

$$y' = 1 - \frac{1}{2x}$$

and it follows that

$$x = x_0 - \frac{x_0 - \frac{1}{2} \ln x_0 - 3}{1 - \frac{1}{2x_0}} = \frac{\ln x_0 + 5}{2 - \frac{1}{x_0}} \tag{13}$$

The program is

```
0    LRN                                                    000

1    ST001 ln x + 5 = ÷ ( 2 − RCL01 1/x ) = R/S   RST    017

     LRN
```

As in section 1, we start with the estimate $x_0 = 3.6$. The input/output procedure is identical to that used with the first program of this section. We obtain the sequence

3.6   3.6470   3.64694490

In this example the Newton-Raphson method is again much more efficient than the simple iteration method.

The alternate method in which nothing is stored works well only for very simple expressions like (11). For more complicated expressions it is usually less efficient than the straightforward procedure, and often does not work at all. Consider equation (13). We rewrite this as

$$x = \frac{\ln \dfrac{1}{x_0} - 5}{\dfrac{1}{x_0} - 2}$$

This can be evaluated by the following program:

0   LRN   000

1    $\dfrac{1}{x} - 2 = \dfrac{1}{x} \times \left(\left(CE \dfrac{1}{x} + 2 \right) \ln x - 5 \right) =$ R/S   RST   020

     LRN

In this case the alternate program is less efficient than the original one. However, it does provide an opportunity to introduce a new programming technique which is occasionally useful. The CE statement can be used to pull the number in the display register inside the parentheses.

We again consider equation (7), which is

$$y = \tan x - x = 0$$

then

$$y' = \tan^2 x$$

and it follows that

$$x = x_0 - \frac{\tan x_0 - x_0}{\tan^2 x_0} = \frac{x_0}{\sin^2 x_0} - \frac{1}{\tan x_0} \qquad (14)$$

The program is

0   LRN   000

1   STO01   2nd Rad ÷ 2nd sin x² — RCL01   2nd tan

$\frac{1}{x}$ = R/S   RST   014

LRN

As in section 1, we start with the estimate $x_0 = 4.4$. The input/output procedure is identical to that used with the first program of this section. We obtain the sequence

4.4   4.536   4.5019   4.49375   4.4934100
4.493409458

In this example the Newton-Raphson method is not much more efficient than the simple iteration method.

The Newton-Raphson method is shown graphically in Fig. 5. The desired root x is estimated and the tangent is drawn to the curve $y = f(x)$ at that point. The intersection of the tangent with the x axis provides a better estimate of the root. The process is repeated as often as necessary until the desired accuracy is obtained.

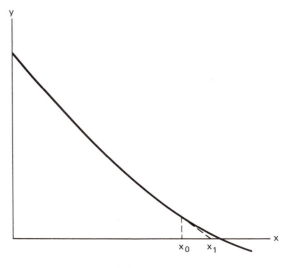

FIGURE 5

Many difficulties can occur in using any numerical method. Sometimes a process is inherently unstable for a particular equation. In other cases the difficulty is caused by a poor initial estimate of the root. We rework the last example, this time starting with the poor initial guess $x_0 = 4.2$. Then we obtain the sequence

4.2   4.97   5.56   13.9

48

It is clear that the process diverges. The stability of the Newton-Raphson method is more sensitive to the initial error than that of the simple iteration method; the latter method converged for this problem even with the very poor initial guess $x_0 = 4.0$.

3. The secant method

Geometrically the Newton-Raphson method consists of making a first estimate of x and then obtaining an improved value by drawing the tangent and extrapolating it to the x axis. A commonly used alternative method is to choose two points that bracket the exact root, then draw the chord connecting them and take the intersection with the x axis as the result, as shown in Fig. 6. This is known as the secant method. It is essentially a form of linear interpolation. The equation is

$$x = \frac{x_1 y_2 - x_2 y_1}{y_2 - y_1} \tag{15}$$

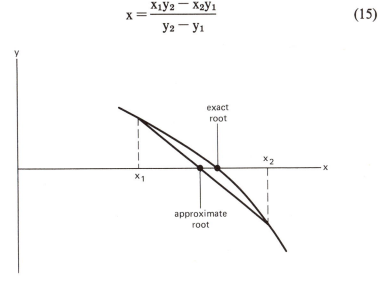

FIGURE 6

The process is repeated as many times as desired. The last and next to last previous values of x and y are used as the starting points for each new cycle. The program for this method is more complicated than those used previously, and the method is somewhat less efficient than the Newton-Raphson method. The major advantage of the method is that the calculations are entirely automatic—no preliminary calculus and algebra are required.

We again start with equation (3), which is

$$y = x^2 - 2x - 4 = 0$$

0	LRN	000
1	SBR045 ST003	005
2	RCL01 2nd Exc 02 STO01	011
3	SBR045 2nd Exc 03 STO04	018
4	RCL01 × RCL04 − RCL02 × RCL03 =	030
5	÷ (RCL04 − RCL03) = STO02 R/S GTO005	045
6	RCL01 − 2 = × RCL01 − 4 = INV SBR	057
	LRN	

The program appears above. The exchange procedure of chapter 1, section 5, is used. The easiest way to see how the program works is to follow through the contents of the data registers at the end of each line of the first two cycles as shown below. The results for the second cycle can be extended indefinitely to higher cycles by adding 1 to the subscripts for each additional cycle. It can be seen that y is calculated twice in the first cycle. This is necessary because the data registers 03 and 04 are initially empty. For each subsequent cycle only one new y is calculated; the transfer statement GTO005 in line 5 skips line 1. The last and next to last previous values of x and y are used as the starting values for each new cycle.

Contents of data registers

first cycle				*second cycle*			
01	02	03	04	01	02	03	04
1 x_1	x_2	y_1					
2 x_2	x_1	y_1		x_3	x_2	y_2	y_1
3 x_2	x_1	y_2	y_1	x_3	x_2	y_3	y_2
5 x_2	x_3	y_2	y_1	x_3	x_4	y_3	y_2

The use of a subroutine in this program has two advantages. The specific equation being solved appears only once, in line 6. Without the subroutine it would have to be written out twice, in lines 1 and 3. A more important advantage is that it appears at the end of the program instead of the beginning. The basic first five lines of the program are entirely general; this segment can be applied as it stands to any other equation. It is only necessary to rewrite line 6 each time. This is much more convenient than rewriting the entire program every time it is used.

The input/output operation is

Press x_1 STO01 x_2 STO02   RST   R/S   R/S   R/S

Display x_3 x_4 x_5

By choosing the starting values $x_1 = 3.2$, $x_2 = 3.3$, we obtain the following sequence of approximations

3.2   3.3   3.2356   3.2360608   3.23606798

The input procedure can be made a little neater by using labels. An alternate program with labels appears below:

0 LRN		000
1 2nd Lbl A STO01 R/S		005
2 2nd Lbl B STO02 SBR054 STO03		014
3 RCL01 2nd Exc 02 STO01		020
4 SBR054 2nd Exc 03 STO04		027
5 RCL01 × RCL04 − RCL02 × RCL03 =		039
6 ÷ (RCL04 − RCL03) = STO02 R/S GTO014		054
7 RCL01 − 2 = × RCL01 − 4 = INV SBR		066
LRN		

The input/output operation is

Press x_1 A x_2 B   R/S   R/S

Display x_3 x_4 x_5

Numerical results are identical to those given by the first program.

With the foregoing program still in the calculator, we can proceed to solve any other equation. We press GTO 054 LRN, followed by the new subroutine and another LRN statement. As a second example we again use equation (5), which is

$$y = x - \frac{1}{2} \ln x - 3 = 0$$

The subroutine is

7 RCL01 − ln x ÷ 2 − 3 = INV SBR   064

The input/output procedure is the same as in the preceding example. Starting with the values $x_1 = 3.6$, $x_2 = 3.7$, we obtain the sequence

3.6   3.7   3.64689   3.6469448   3.64694490

As a third example we again use equation (7), which is

$$y = \tan x - x = 0$$

The subroutine is

7   2nd Rad   RCL01 − 2nd tan = INV SBR   061

We start with the values $x_1 = 4.4$, $x_2 = 4.6$. The results are

4.4   4.6   4.447   4.470   4.4985
4.4928   4.49340   4.4934095   4.493409458

The initial iteration in the secant method as depicted in Fig. 6 is an interpolation. Subsequent results may be either interpolations or extrapolations. If successive results oscillate about the true value, each iteration is an interpolation between a high and a low estimate. However, an inspection of the results of the foregoing examples shows that it is also possible for results to approach the exact value from one side. In this case the method is an extrapolation process rather than an interpolation process.

In all three examples the secant method has a longer running time than the Newton-Raphson method; the program is longer and the convergence is somewhat slower. However, the program is fully automatic—no preliminary calculus and algebra are required.

Problems

Solve equations 1 through 10 numerically. (Answers are given to make it easy to check the numerical evaluations.)

1. $x^3 - 4x^2 + 3x + 1 = 0$
    $x = -.24697\ 96037, \quad 1.44504\ 1868, \quad 2.80193\ 7736$

2. $x^4 - x^3 - 3x^2 + 2x + 2 = 0 \quad x = \sqrt{2}, \frac{1}{2}(1 \pm \sqrt{5})$

3. $x^4 + x^3 - 7x^2 - 4x + 6 = 0 \quad x = -1 \pm \sqrt{3}, \frac{1}{2}(1 \pm \sqrt{13})$

4. $x^3 - 18.1x - 34.8 = 0$
    $x = 5.00526\ 5097, \quad -2.50263\ 2549 \pm .83036\ 800i$

5. $x^4 - 3x^3 + 6x^2 - 3x - 5 = 0 \quad x = \frac{1}{2}(1 \pm \sqrt{5}), 1 \pm 2i$

6. $x^4 - 5x^3 + 11x^2 - 14x + 4 = 0 \quad x = \frac{1}{2}(3 \pm \sqrt{5}), 1 \pm i\sqrt{3}$

7. $x + \ln x = 5 \quad x = 3.69344\ 1359$

8. $3x - 4 \sin x = 2 \quad x = 1.91967\ 5341$

9. $e^{-x} + \sin x - 5x + 2 = 0 \quad x = .62401\ 75637$

10. $e^x = (5 - x)^3 \quad x = 2.61172\ 0144$

11. Use the Newton-Raphson method to evaluate $\sqrt{5}$.   Ans. 2.23606 7978

12. Use the Newton-Raphson method to evaluate $\sqrt[3]{5}$.   Ans. 1.70997 5947

13. Find the smallest positive nonzero root of the equation $\tan x = 2x$.   Ans. $x = 1.16556\ 1185$

3

SOME HIGHER TRANSCENDENTAL FUNCTIONS

The elementary trigonometric, exponential, and logarithmic functions are provided with the calculator. When more advanced functions are required, it is necessary to write programs for them. In this chapter programs are developed for a number of commonly occurring higher transcendental functions.

1. The sine integral and the cosine integral

The sine integral Si(x) is defined by the equation

$$Si(x) = \int_0^x \frac{\sin t}{t}\, dt \tag{1}$$

By expanding the integrand into an infinite series and integrating term by term, we find that

$$Si(x) = x - \frac{x^3}{3 \cdot 3!} + \frac{x^5}{5 \cdot 5!} - \frac{x^7}{7 \cdot 7!} + \ldots \tag{2}$$

There are several possible nested forms of this equation. The most convenient one is

$$Si(x) = x \left(1 - \frac{1x^2}{2 \cdot 3^2} \left(1 - \frac{3x^2}{4 \cdot 5^2} \left(1 - \frac{5x^2}{6 \cdot 7^2} \left(1 - \ldots \right) \right) \right) \right) \tag{3}$$

The number of terms n needed to obtain satisfactory convergence depends upon the value of x. It is desirable to include an automatic provision in the program to determine the appropriate value of n, rather than try several values manually for each value of x. Results are accurate to the full extent of the calculator display provided that n is given by the equation

$$n = 1.5x + 6 \tag{4}$$

rounded off to the next lower integer.

The numerical evaluation is given in the program below. Line 1 represents equation (4).* The 1 at the end of this line is the 1 at the extreme right of equation (3). Lines 2 and 3 constitute a Dsz

---

* These expressions differ by 1 because the number of cycles in the Dsz loop is 1 less than the number of terms considered when the nested series (3) is used.

loop which evaluates the nested series on the right side of equation (3), proceeding from right to left and ending with the 1 inside the left parenthesis. Line 4 performs the final multiplication by x and displays the result.

0	LRN	000
1	STO01 × 1.5 + 5 = 2nd Int STO02 1	013
2	× RCL01 x² × (RCL02 − .5) ÷ RCL02	028
3	÷ (2 × RCL02 + 1) x² +/− + 1 = 2nd Dsz 2013	046
4	× RCL01 = R/S	051
	LRN	

Contents of data registers

01 x   02 n − 1, n − 2, ... , 1

Input/output

Press   x   RST   R/S

Display   Si(x)

Accurate numerical results from reference 3 appear in the table below. Results from the program are identical to those shown.

x	$Si(x)$	x	$Si(x)$	x	$Si(x)$
0	0.00000 0000	4	1.75820 3139	8	1.57418 6822
1	0.94608 3070	5	1.54993 1245	9	1.66504 0076
2	1.60541 2977	6	1.42468 7551	10	1.65834 7594
3	1.84865 2528	7	1.45459 6614		

The cosine integral Ci(x) is defined by the equation

$$Ci(x) = -\int_{x}^{\infty} \frac{\cos t}{t}\, dt \tag{5}$$

In this case the series expansion is not elementary. It can be shown that*

$$Ci(x) = \gamma + \ln x - \frac{x^2}{2 \cdot 2!} + \frac{x^4}{4 \cdot 4!} - \frac{x^6}{6 \cdot 6!} + \ldots \qquad (6)$$

where γ is Euler's constant. The nested form of this equation is

$$Ci(x) = \gamma + \ln x - \frac{x^2}{4}\left(1 - \frac{2x^2}{3 \cdot 4^2}\left(1 - \frac{4x^2}{5 \cdot 6^2}\left(1 - \ldots\right)\right)\right)$$

$$Ci(x) = \gamma + \ln x - \frac{x^2}{4}\left(1 - \frac{1x^2}{6 \cdot 2^2}\left(1 - \frac{2x^2}{10 \cdot 3^2}\left(1 - \ldots\right)\right)\right) \qquad (7)$$

Results are accurate to the full extent of the calculator display if n is given by equation (4), again rounded off to the next lower integer.

The numerical evaluation is given in the program below. This is organized in the same way as the program for the sine integral given previously.

0   LRN   000

1   ST001 × 1.5 + 5 = 2nd Int   ST002   1   013

2   × RCL01 x² × RCL02 ÷ (4 × RCL02 + 2)   029

3   ÷ (RCL02 + 1) x² +/− + 1 = 2nd Dsz 2013   045

4   × RCL01 x² ÷ 4 +/− + RCL01 ln x +
    .57721 56649 = R/S   070

    LRN

Contents of data registers

01 x 02 n − 1, n − 2, ... , 1

Input/output

---

* All of the algorithms used in this chapter can be found in reference 3, unless other references are cited. Derivations can be found in reference 5.

Press x RST R/S

Display Ci(x)

Accurate numerical results from reference 3 appear in the table below. Results from the program are identical to those shown.

x	Ci(x)	x	Ci(x)	x	Ci(x)
1	.33740 39229	5	−.19002 97497	9	−.05534 75313
2	.42298 08288	6	−.06805 72439	10	−.04545 64330
3	.11962 97860	7	.07669 52785		
4	−.14098 16979	8	.12243 38825		

2. The exponential integrals

The exponential integral Ei(x) is defined by the equation

$$\text{Ei}(x) = -\int_{-x}^{\infty} \frac{e^{-t}}{t}\, dt \qquad (8)$$

The series expansion is

$$\text{Ei}(x) = \gamma + \ln x + \frac{x}{1 \cdot 1!} + \frac{x^2}{2 \cdot 2!} + \frac{x^3}{3 \cdot 3!} + \dots \qquad (9)$$

In nested form, this becomes

$$\text{Ei}(x) = \gamma + \ln x + x\left(1 + \frac{1x}{2^2}\left(1 + \frac{2x}{3^2}\left(1 + \frac{3x}{4^2}\left(1 + \dots\right)\right)\right)\right) \qquad (10)$$

Results are accurate to the full extent of the calculator display if the number of terms n is given by the equation

$$n = 2.3x + 12 \qquad (11)$$

rounded off to the next lower integer.

The numerical evaluation is given in the program below. Line 1 represents equation (11). The 1 at the end of this line is the 1 at the extreme right of equation (10). Line 2 constitutes a Dsz loop that evaluates the nested series on the right side of equation (10).

The calculation proceeds from right to left and ends with the 1 inside the first parenthesis. Line 3 completes the evaluation of Ei(x). This will ordinarily be the last line of the program. Line 4 calculates the function $xe^{-x}Ei(x)$ which is needed for comparison with accurate results from reference 3.

0	LRN	000
1	STO01 × 2.3 + 11 = 2nd Int STO02 1	014
2	× RCL01 × RCL02 ÷ (RCL02 + 1) x² + 1 = 2nd Dsz 2014	035
3	× RCL01 + RCL01 ln x + .57721 56649 = R/S	056
4	÷ RCL01 INV ln x × RCL01 = R/S	066
	LRN	

Contents of data registers

01 x   02 n − 1, n − 2, ... , 1

Input/output

Press   x   RST   R/S   R/S

Display   Ei(x)   xe⁻ˣEi(x)

Accurate numerical results from reference 3 appear in the table below. Results from the program are identical to those shown, with the exception of some slight discrepancies in the last digit.

x	$x\,e^{-x}\,Ei(x)$	x	$xe^{-x}\,Ei(x)$	x	$xe^{-x}\,Ei(x)$
1	0.69717 4883	5	1.35383 1278	9	1.15275 9209
2	1.34096 5420	6	1.27888 3860	10	1.13147 0205
3	1.48372 9204	7	1.22240 8053		
4	1.43820 8032	8	1.18184 7987		

The exponential integral $E_1(x)$ is defined by the equation

$$E_1(x) = \int_x^\infty \frac{e^{-t}}{t} \, dt \qquad (12)$$

This integral is more difficult to evaluate numerically than the ones which we have considered previously. The most commonly used series expansion is

$$E_1(x) = -\gamma - \ln x + \frac{x}{1 \cdot 1!} - \frac{x^2}{2 \cdot 2!} + \frac{x^3}{3 \cdot 3!} - \ldots \qquad (13)$$

that is obtained from the integral representation

$$E_1(x) = -\gamma - \ln x + \int_0^x \frac{1 - e^{-t}}{t} \, dt$$

It is difficult to obtain accurate results from equation (13) unless x is small, because $E_1(x)$ approaches zero rapidly as x becomes large. At the same time the individual terms of the series become numerically large and alternately positive and negative. Hence the desired result is the small difference of large terms, and is subject to a large roundoff error. Equation (13) is suitable for use in a computer with double precision. For a pocket calculator it is better to rewrite the integral representation as

$$E_1(x) = -\gamma - \ln x + e^{-x} \int_0^x \frac{e^x - e^{x-t}}{t} \, dt$$

This generates the series

$$E_1(x) = -\gamma - \ln x + e^{-x}(a_1 x + a_2 x^2 + a_3 x^3 + \ldots) \qquad (14)$$

The coefficients are given by the equation

$$a_i = \frac{1}{i!}\left(1 + \frac{1}{2} + \frac{1}{3} + \ldots + \frac{1}{i}\right) \qquad (15)$$

This can be evaluated as it stands, but a result with a slightly smaller roundoff error is obtained by a different procedure. We write

$$a_i = \frac{c_i}{(i!)^2} \qquad (16)$$

61

The first few c's are

$$c_1 = 1 \quad c_2 = 3 \quad c_3 = 11 \quad c_4 = 50 \quad c_5 = 274$$

It is easy to show that the c's are given by the recurrence relation

$$c_i = ic_{i-1} + (i-1)! \tag{17}$$

Full convergence is obtained provided that n is given by the equation

$$n = 2.5x + 16 \tag{18}$$

rounded off to the next lower integer.

If we write the series (14) in nested form, a slight difficulty arises. A nested series is evaluated from right to left. As a result we would need a_n, a_{n-1}, a_{n-2}, ... in that order. However, equations (16) and (17) give the c's and a's in ascending order, starting with c_1. There are several possible ways to work your way around this difficulty, but the simplest procedure is to abandon the nested format and sum the series (14) directly from left to right. The numerical evaluation is given in the program below. Line 1 represents equation (18) and line 2 stores the appropriate starting values of the parameters. Lines 3 through 5 constitute a Dsz loop which evaluates the series in parentheses in equation (14). Line 3 calculates c_1, line 4 evaluates i! and x^i, and line 5 completes the evaluation of the series. Line 6 completes the evaluation of $E_1(x)$. In most applications this will be the last line of the program. Line 7 evaluates $xe^{-x}E_1(x)$, which is needed to check the program against available tabular results from reference 3.

0	LRN	000
1	ST001 × 2.5 + 16 = 2nd Int ST003	013
2	0 ST004 ST006 ST008 1 ST005 ST007	025
3	2nd Op 24 RCL04 2nd Prd 06 RCL05 SUM06	035
4	RCL04 2nd Prd 05 RCL01 2nd Prd 07	043
5	RCL06 ÷ RCL05 x^2 × RCL07 = SUM08 2nd Dsz 3025	059

6   RCL08 ÷ RCL01 INV ln x — RCL01 ln x —
    RCL02   = R/S   075

7   × RCL01 INV ln x × RCL01 = R/S   085

    LRN

Contents of data registers at end of i th cycle

01 x   02 γ 03 n − 1   04 i   05 i!   06 c_i 07 x^i 08
partial sum

There are two input parameters. The value of x is stored in data
register 01. This is done in line 1 of the program. Euler's constant
$\gamma = .5772156649015$ is stored in data register 02. This is done in
the input/output operation. Because of the importance of roundoff
error, 13 digits must be inserted using the procedure of chapter 1,
section 7. The input/output procedure is

Press   577 + .21566 49015 = ÷ 1000 = STO02
                                    x   RST   R/S   R/S

Display $E_1(x)$ x $e^x E_1(x)$

The value of γ is inserted only once. If the program is used for more
than one value of x, results after the first are obtained by pressing

x   RST   R/S   R/S.

Accurate numerical results from reference 3 appear in the table
below. Results from the program are shown for comparison. The error
is negligible provided that x ≤ 8.

	$xe^x E_1(x)$		
x	Reference 3	Program	Asymptotic Program
2	.72265 7234	7234	
4	.82538 2600	2596	
6	.87160 5775	5764	
8	.89823 7113	6987	8205
10	.91563 3339	1703	3304

If $x > 8$, better results are obtained from the asymptotic formula

$$xe^x E_1(x) = \frac{x^2 + 4.0364x + 1.15198}{x^2 + 5.03637x + 4.1916} \tag{19}$$

The program follows.

```
0   LRN                                              000

1   STO01 + 4.0364 = × RCL01 + 1.15198 =             022

2   ÷(RCL01 × (RCL01 + 5.03637) + 4.1916) =          048

3   STO02 ÷ RCL01 ÷ RCL01INV ln x = R/S              060

    LRN
```

Contents of data registers

01 x   02 $x\,e^x E_1(x)$

Input/output

Press   x   RST   R/S   RCL02

Display $E_1(x)$ $x\,e^x E_1(x)$

Numerical results appear in the last column of the foregoing table.

3. The error function

The error function erf x is defined by the equation

$$\text{erf } x = \frac{2}{\sqrt{\pi}} \int_0^x e^{-t^2}\, dt \tag{20}$$

By expanding the integrand into an infinite series and integrating term by term, we find that

$$\text{erf } x = \frac{2}{\sqrt{\pi}} \, x \left(1 - \frac{x^2}{3 \cdot 1!} + \frac{x^4}{5 \cdot 2!} - \frac{x^6}{7 \cdot 3!} + \frac{x^8}{9 \cdot 4!} - \cdots \right) \quad (21)$$

The shortest program is obtained by using a slightly different type of nested equation from those used previously. Thus

$$\text{erf } x = \frac{2}{\sqrt{\pi}} \, x \left(1 - x^2 \left(\frac{1}{3} - \frac{x^2}{2} \left(\frac{1}{5} - \frac{x^2}{3} \left(\frac{1}{7} - \frac{x^2}{4} \left(\frac{1}{9} - \cdots \right) \right) \right) \right) \right) \quad (22)$$

Results are accurate to the full extent of the calculator display provided that the number of terms n is given by the equation

$$n = 12x + 3 \qquad (23)$$

rounded off to the next lower integer.

The numerical evaluation of erf x appears in the program below. Line 1 represents equation (23). The last entry in this line is the number at the extreme right of equation (22). Line 2 constitutes a Dsz loop which evaluates the nested series on the right side of equation (22). The calculation proceeds from right to left and ends with the 1 inside the first parenthesis. Line 3 completes the evaluation of erf x.

0 LRN   000

1 STO01 × 12 + 2 = 2nd Int   STO02 × 2 + 1 = $\frac{1}{x}$ 017

2   × RCL01 x² ÷ RCL02+/− + (2 × RCL02 − 1) $\frac{1}{x}$ =

    2nd Dsz 2017   040

3   × RCL01 × 2 ÷ 2nd π $\sqrt{x}$ = R/S   050

         LRN

Contents of data registers

01 x   02 n − 1, n − 2, ... , 1

Input/output

Press x RST R/S

Display   erf x

Accurate numerical results from reference 4 appear in the table below. Results from the program are identical to those shown with the exception of some slight discrepancies in the last digit. For larger values of x, erf x is usually taken as 1.

x	$erf\ x$	x	$erf\ x$
0.0	.00000 00000	2.0	.99532 22650
0.5	.52049 98778	2.5	.99959 30480
1.0	.84270 07929	3.0	.99997 79095
1.5	.96610 51465	3.5	.99999 92569

4. Complete elliptic integrals

The complete elliptic integral of the first kind $K(k)$ is defined by the equation

$$K(k) = \int_0^{\pi/2} \frac{d\theta}{(1 - k^2 \sin^2 \theta)^{1/2}} \tag{24}$$

The best way to evaluate this integral numerically is to use the infinite product (reference 7)

$$K(k) = \frac{\pi}{2}(1 + k_1)(1 + k_2)(1 + k_3)\ldots \tag{25}$$

The k's are given by the recurrence relation

$$k_i = \frac{1 - \sqrt{1 - k_{i-1}^2}}{1 + \sqrt{1 - k_{i-1}^2}} \qquad k_0 = k \tag{26}$$

This can be simplified to either

$$k_i = \left(\frac{1 - \sqrt{1 - k_{i-1}^2}}{k_{i-1}}\right)^2 \qquad k_0 = k \tag{27}$$

$$k_i = \left(\frac{k_{i-1}}{1 + \sqrt{1 - k_{i-1}^2}}\right)^2 \qquad k_0 = k \qquad (28)$$

The last form is preferable because it does not break down when $k = 0$. Results are accurate to the full extent of the calculator display provided that $k^2 \leq .99$ and five terms are taken in the infinite product (25).

The program appears below. Line 1 stores the starting values of the parameters. Lines 2 and 3 constitute a Dsz loop; line 2 evaluates k_i by equation (28), and line 3 evaluates $K(k)$ by equation (25).

0   LRN   000

1   STO01   5 STO02   2nd $\pi \div 2 =$ STO03   011

2   RCL01 x² +/− + 1 = $\sqrt{x}$ + 1 = $\dfrac{1}{x}$ × RCL01 = x²

    STO01   030

3   +1 = 2nd Prd 03   2nd Dsz 2011   RCL03   R/S   042

    LRN

Contents of data registers at end of i th cycle

01 k_i 02 5 − i   03 $\dfrac{\pi}{2}$ $(1 + k_1)(1 + k_2) \ldots (1 + k_i)$

Input/output

Press   k   RST   R/S

Display   K(k)

Accurate numerical results from reference 3 are given in the table at the end of this section. Results from the program are identical to those shown. The integral (24) diverges when $k = 1$.

The complete elliptic integral of the second kind E(k) is defined by the equation

$$E(k) = \int_0^{\pi/2} (1 - k^2 \sin^2 \theta)^{1/2} \, d\theta \qquad (29)$$

This is evaluated numerically by using the expansion

$$E(k) = K(k) \left[1 - \frac{k^2}{2}\left(1 + \frac{k_1}{2} + \frac{k_1}{2}\frac{k_2}{2} + \frac{k_1}{2}\frac{k_2}{2}\frac{k_3}{2} + \ldots \right) \right] \qquad (30)$$

As we observed in section 2, a nested form of this series is not practical because the k's must be found from a recurrence formula.

The program follows. Since the value of K(k) is needed as an intermediate step in the evaluation of E(k), the program calculates both. When this program is used, the earlier program is not needed. Line 1 stores the starting values of the parameters. Lines 2 and 3 constitute a Dsz loop. Line 2 calculates k_1; line 3 calculates K(k) and evaluates the expression in parentheses in equation (30). Line 4 recalls K(k) and completes the evaluation of E(k).

0   LRN   000

1   ST001   ST003   5 ST002   2nd $\pi \div 2 =$ ST004
    1 ST005   ST006   018

2   RCL03 x^2 +/− + 1 = $\sqrt{x}$ + 1 = $\dfrac{1}{x}$ × RCL03 =

    x^2 ST003   037

3   + 1 = 2nd Prd 04 − 1 = ÷ 2 = 2nd Prd 05   RCL05
    SUM06   2nd Dsz 2018   058

4   RCL04   R/S   ×(1 − RCL01 x^2 × RCL06 ÷ 2) =
    R/S   076

    LRN

Contents of data registers at end of i th cycle

01 k   02 5−i   03 k_i 04 $\dfrac{\pi}{2}$ $(1 + k_1)(1 + k_2)$. . . .

$$05 \frac{k_1}{2} \frac{k_2}{2} \cdots \qquad 06\ 1 + \frac{k_1}{2} + \frac{k_1}{2} \frac{k_2}{2} + \cdots$$

Input/output

Press   k   RST   R/S   R/S

Display   K(k)   E(k)

Accurate numerical results from reference 3 are given below. Results from the program are identical to those shown. The integral (29) converges to the value 1 when k = 1, but the expansion (30) breaks down.

k^2	$K(k)$	$E(k)$	k^2	$K(k)$	$E(k)$
0.0	1.57079 6327	1.57079 6327	0.6	1.94956 7750	1.29842 8034
.1	1.61244 1349	1.53075 7637	.7	2.07536 3135	1.24167 0567
.2	1.65962 3599	1.48903 5058	.8	2.25720 5327	1.17848 9924
.3	1.71388 9448	1.44536 3064	.9	2.57809 2113	1.10477 4733
.4	1.77751 9371	1.39939 2139	.99	3.69563 7363	1.01599 3546
.5	1.85407 4677	1.35064 3881			

5.   The factorial function

The factorial function x! is defined by the equation*

$$x! = \int_0^\infty t^x\, e^{-t}\, dt \tag{31}$$

By integrating by parts k times, we find that

$$x! = x(x-1)(x-2) \cdots (x-k+1) \int_0^\infty t^{x-k}\, e^{-t}\, dt$$
$$= x(x-1)(x-2) \cdots (x-k+1)[(x-k)!] \tag{32}$$

If x is an integer, we set k = x. Then this reduces to the elementary factorial. A program to evaluate the elementary factorial has been

* The Gamma function is also used. This is defined by the equation

$$\Gamma(x) = (x-1)! = \int_0^\infty t^{x-1}\, e^{-t}\, dt$$

given in chapter 1, section 3. The easiest way to evaluate x! in the general case is to use the asymptotic formula

$$\ln x! = \left(x + \frac{1}{2}\right)\ln x - x + \frac{1}{2}\ln 2\pi - \frac{1}{12x}\left(1 - \frac{1}{30x^2}\right.$$
$$\left. + \frac{1}{105x^4} - \frac{1}{140x^6} + \frac{1}{99x^8} - \ldots\right) \quad (33)$$

This can be written in nested form as

$$\ln x! = \left(x + \frac{1}{2}\right)\ln x - x + \frac{1}{2}\ln 2\pi + \frac{1}{12x}\left(1 - \frac{1}{x^2}\left(\frac{1}{30}\right.\right.$$
$$\left.\left. - \frac{1}{x^2}\left(\frac{1}{105} - \frac{1}{x^2}\left(\frac{1}{140} - \frac{1}{x^2}\left(\frac{1}{99}\right)\right)\right)\right)\right) \quad (34)$$

Equation (34) is very good for large values of x. For x ≥ 5, it gives results that are accurate to the full extent of the calculator display. For smaller values of x, results are obtained by using equation (32) in conjunction with (34). Thus, for example

$$1.3! = \frac{5.3!}{5.3 \cdot 4.3 \cdot 3.3 \cdot 2.3}$$

The program appears below. The starting values of the parameters are stored in line 1. In lines 2 and 3 the parameter x is tested to see whether it ≥ 5. If it is less than 5, it is incremented by 1 and again checked. This process is repeated as many times as necessary until the final incremented value ≥ 5. At the same time the product (x + 1)(x + 2). . . . is collected in data register 02. In lines 4 through 9, the factorial function of the incremented parameter is calculated from equation (34). This is then divided by the product stored in data register 02. The final result is x! A Dsz loop has not been used because the coefficients in equation (34) are not given by any simple rule. The indirect addressing scheme of chapter 1, section 6, could have been used, but in this problem it is easier to write out the whole program.

0	LRN		000

1	ST001	1 ST002	005

2 5 x ⇌ t   RCL01   2nd x ≥ t021   2nd Op 21   014

3 RCL01   2nd Prd 02   GTO005   021

4 99 $\frac{1}{x}$ ÷ RCL01 x² +/− + 140 $\frac{1}{x}$ =   035

5   ÷ RCL01 x² +/− + 105 $\frac{1}{x}$ =   046

6   ÷ RCL01 x² + / − + 30 $\frac{1}{x}$ =   056

7   ÷ RCL01 x² + / − + 1 =   064

8   ÷ RCL01 ÷ 12 + (2 × 2nd π) ln x ÷ 2 −
    RCL01 + RCL01 ln x × (RCL01 + .5) =   095

9   INV ln x ÷ RCL02 = R/S   102

    LRN

Contents of data registers

01 x   02 (x + 1)(x + 2). . . .

Input/output

Press   x   RST   R/S

Display   x!

This program can be used for any real value of x, positive or negative, provided that x is not a negative integer, in which case x! is infinite. Results are accurate to the full extent of the calculator display.

6. Bessel functions

Bessel functions occur in many applications in science and engineering. The series expansion for the Bessel function of the first kind $J_\nu(x)$ is

$$J_\nu(x) = \frac{1}{\nu!}\left(\frac{x}{2}\right)^\nu\left[1 - \frac{\left(\frac{x}{2}\right)^2}{(\nu+1)1!} + \frac{\left(\frac{x}{2}\right)^4}{(\nu+1)(\nu+2)2!} - \cdots\right] \quad (35)$$

where x is any real positive number and ν is any real number except a negative integer. In nested form this becomes

$$J_\nu(x) = \frac{1}{\nu!}\left(\frac{x}{2}\right)^\nu\left(1 - \frac{\left(\frac{x}{2}\right)^2}{1(\nu+1)}\left(1 - \frac{\left(\frac{x}{2}\right)^2}{2(\nu+2)}\left(1 - \cdots\right)\right)\right) \quad (36)$$

Results are accurate to the full extent of the calculator display provided that the number of terms n is given by the equation

$$n = 2x + 5 \quad (37)$$

rounded off to the next lower integer.

Most of the length of a complete program for $J_\nu(x)$ is taken up by the evaluation of the factorial function. The series alone can be evaluated by a simple program similar to the one written for the sine integral in section 1. Let $S_\nu(x) = \nu!J_\nu(x)$. A program for $S_\nu(x)$ follows:

```
0   LRN                                              000

1   2nd Lbl A   STO02   R/S                          005

2   2nd Lbl B ÷ 2 = STO01 × 4 + 4 = 2nd Int
    STO03   1                                        021

3   × RCL01 x² ÷ RCL03 ÷ (RCL02 +
    RCL03) +/− + 1 = 2nd Dsz 3021                    044

4   × RCL01 yˣ RCL02 = R/S                           052

    LRN
```

Contents of data registers

$01 \dfrac{x}{2}$ 02ν $03 \ n-i$

Input/output

Press ν A x B

Display $S_\nu(x)$

The foregoing program is adequate for the solution of most practical problems involving Bessel functions. Usually the factorial functions cancel or occur in combinations which cancel. Two typical problems involving Bessel functions are

$$J_{1/4}(x) = 0 \qquad y = \frac{J_{1/4}(x)}{J_{-3/4}(x)}$$

These can be reduced to the equivalent forms

$$S_{1/4}(x) = 0 \qquad y = 4\frac{S_{1/4}(x)}{S_{-3/4}(x)}$$

When ν is a positive integer, say $\nu = p$, a segment to evaluate $1/p!$ can easily be annexed to the basic program. (We actually calculate $(p + 1)/(p + 1)!$, so the program will not break down when p = 0.) The program for $J_p(x)$ is

0	LRN	000
1	2nd Lbl A STO02 R/S	005
2	2nd Lbl B ÷ 2 = STO01 × 4 + 4 = 2nd Int STO03 1	021
3	× RCL01 x² ÷ RCL03 ÷ (RCL02 + RCL03) +/− + 1 = 2nd Dsz 3021	044
4	× RCL01 yˣ RCL02 = 2nd Op 22 × RCL02	056
5	÷ RCL02 = 2nd Dsz 2056 R/S	065
	LRN	

Numerical results are given in the table below for several values of p and x. These are taken from reference 3. Results from the program are identical to those shown with the exception of some slight discrepancies in the last digit.

x	$J_0(x)$	$J_1(x)$	$J_2(x)$
0	1.00000 00000	0.00000 00000	0.00000 00000
2	.22389 07791	.57672 48078	.35283 40286
4	−.39714 98099	−.06604 33280	.36412 81459
6	.15064 52573	−.27668 38581	−.24287 32100
8	.17165 08071	.23463 63469	−.11299 17204
10	−.24593 5765	.04347 27462	.25463 03137

If a complete evaluation of $J_\nu(x)$ is needed for a nonintegral value of ν, this can be obtained by using the first program of this section in conjunction with the factorial program of section 5. The two programs can easily be combined if desired, but a combined program is seldom needed.

When ν is a positive integer, say $\nu = p$, it is sometimes necessary to use the Bessel function of the second kind as well as the Bessel function of the first kind. The Bessel function of the second kind $Y_p(x)$ is given by the formula

$$Y_p(x) = \frac{1}{\pi}\left[2\left(\ln \frac{x}{2} - \gamma \right) J_p(x) - M_p(x) - N_p(x) \right] \tag{38}$$

where γ is Euler's constant and

$$J_p(x) = \frac{1}{p!}\left(\frac{x}{2} \right)^p \left[1 - \frac{\left(\frac{x}{2} \right)^2}{1 \cdot (p+1)} \right.$$

$$\left. + \frac{\left(\frac{x}{2} \right)^4}{1 \cdot 2 \cdot (p+1)(p+2)} - \cdots \right] \tag{39}$$

$$M_p(x) = \frac{1}{p!}\left(\frac{x}{2} \right)^p \left\{ \phi(p) - [\phi(1) + \phi(p+1)] \frac{\left(\frac{x}{2} \right)^2}{1 \cdot (p+1)} + \cdots \right\} \tag{40}$$

$$N_p(x) = (p-1)! \left(\frac{x}{2}\right)^{-p} \left[1 - \frac{1}{1 \cdot (p-1)} \left(\frac{x}{2}\right)^2 + \frac{1}{1 \cdot 2(p-1(p-2)} \right.$$

$$\left. \left(\frac{x}{2}\right)^4 + \cdots + \frac{1}{1 \cdot 2 \cdot 3 \cdots (p-1)(p-1)!} \left(\frac{x}{2}\right)^{2p-2} \right] \quad (41)$$

The function ϕ is defined by the equation

$$\phi(k) = 1 + \frac{1}{2} + \frac{1}{3} + \cdots + \frac{1}{k} \quad (42)$$

The evaluation of $Y_p(x)$ is much more complicated than the evaluation of $J_p(x)$ given earlier. The series for $M_p(x)$ is not suitable for a nested evaluation; equation (40) is used as it stands. It is convenient to evaluate $J_p(x)$ by equation (39) at the same time, since this equation is the same as (40) except that it does not contain the ϕ functions. $J_p(x)$ and $M_p(x)$ are evaluated in the first 11 lines of the program below. The function $N_p(x)$ is suitable for a nested evaluation. We use the finite series

$$N_p(x) = (p-1)! \left(\frac{x}{2}\right)^{-p} \left[1 + \frac{1}{1(p-1)} \frac{x^2}{4} \left(1 + \frac{1}{2(p-2)} \frac{x^2}{4} \right.\right.$$

$$\left.\left. \cdots \left(1 + \frac{1}{(p-1)!} \frac{x^2}{4} \right) \right) \right] \quad (43)$$

This is evaluated in lines 12 through 15. The general evaluation of the series in brackets that is given in lines 13 and 14 works only when $p \geq 2$. The values 0 for $p = 0$ and 1 for $p = 1$ are inserted separately in line 12. Line 15 completes the evaluation of $N_p(x)$, and line 16 represents equation (38).

```
0   LRN                                              000

1   2nd Lbl A   STO02   STO03   R/S                   007

2   2nd Lbl B ÷ 2 = STO01   1 STO04   STO07
    STO08   STO10   0 STO05                           026

3   RCL02   x ⇌ t   0 2nd x = t 044                   033
```

4   RCL03   2nd Prd 04 $\frac{1}{x}$ SUM05   2nd Dsz 3033   044

5   4 $\times$ RCL01 $+$ 4 $=$ 2nd Int   STO06   RCL05
    STO09   STO11   060

6   RCL07   2nd Prd 08 $+$ RCL02 $= +/-$ 2nd Prd 08   071

7   RCL07 $\frac{1}{x}$ SUM09 $\frac{1}{x}$ $+$ RCL02 $= \frac{1}{x}$ SUM09   084

8   RCL01 y^x RCL07 $= x^2 \div$ RCL08 $=$ SUM10   097

9   $\times$ RCL09 $=$ SUM11   2nd Op 27   2nd Dsz 6060   109

10 RCL10 $\div$ RCL04 $\times$ RCL01 y^x RCL02 $=$ STO12
    R/S   124

11 $\div$ RCL10 $\times$ RCL11 $=$ STO13   133

12 RCL02   x $\rightleftharpoons$ t   0 2nd x $=$ t 186   1 2nd x $=$ t 172   144

13 x $\rightleftharpoons$ t   STO03   2nd Op 33   1   150

14 $\times$ RCL01 $x^2 \div$ RCL03 $\div$ (RCL02 $-$ RCL03) $+$
    1 $=$ 2nd Dsz 3150   172

15 $\times$ RCL04 $\div$ RCL02 $\div$ RCL01 y^x RCL02 $= +/-$ 186

16 $-$ RCL13 $+$ 2 $\times$ RCL12 $\times$ (RCL01 lnx $+$
    .57721 56649) $= \div$ 2nd π $=$ R/S   217

    LRN

Contents of data registers

01 $\frac{x}{2}$ 02 p   03 p, p $-$ 1, p $-$ 2, ... 1   04 p!   05 $\phi(p)$

06 n $-$ 1   07 i   08 i!(p $+$ 1)(p $+$ 2) $\cdots$ (p $+$ i)

09 $\phi(i) + \phi(p + i)$ 10 series for $J_p(x)$

11 series for $M_p(x)$ 12 $J_p(x)$ 13 $M_p(x)$

Input/output

Press   p A   x B   R/S

Display $J_p(x)$ $Y_p(x)$

Some numerical results from the program appear in the table below for $Y_p(x)$. Results given in reference 3 agree with those shown. The values of $J_p(x)$ given by the program are also consistent with those shown earlier. However, the last program is more sensitive to roundoff error than the earlier one. For values of $x > 10$ there is a substantial loss of accuracy in numerical results for $J_p(x)$ from the last program, whereas the earlier program is still reliable. Asymptotic formulas for large values of x can be found in reference 3.

x	$Y_0(x)$	$Y_1(x)$	$Y_2(x)$
2	0.51037 56726	−0.10703 24315	−0.61740 81042
4	− .01694 07393	.39792 57106	.21590 35946
6	− .28819 46840	− .17501 03443	.22985 79025
8	.22352 14894	− .15806 04617	− .26303 66050
10	.05567 11673	.24901 54242	− .00586 80834

Problems

1. Given the identity

$$\int_0^\infty \frac{e^{-xt}}{t^2 + 1}\, dt = \sin x\, Ci(x) + \cos x \left[\frac{\pi}{2} - Si(x) \right]$$

write a program to evaluate the integral. The following results may be used to check the program:

X	I	2	5
I	.62144 96242	.39902 09886	.18814 27746

10
.09819 10348

2. The function $E_n(x)$ is defined by the equation

$$E_n(x) = \int_1^\infty \frac{e^{-xt}}{t^n}\, dt \qquad n = 0,1,2,3, \ldots .$$

Show that $E_0(x) = e^{-x}/x$ and that $E_1(x)$ is consistent with equation (12). Also show that $E_n(x)$ satisfies the recurrence formula

$$E_n(x) = \frac{1}{n-1}[e^{-x} - xE_{n-1}(x)] \qquad n \geq 2$$

Write a program to evaluate $E_n(x)$ for $n \geq 1$. The program can be checked against numerical results given on pages 245–248 of reference 3.

3. By rewriting equation (20) as

$$\text{erf } x = \frac{2}{\sqrt{\pi}} e^{-x^2} \int_0^x e^{x^2-t^2} dt$$

obtain the series expansion

$$\text{erf } x = \frac{2x}{\sqrt{\pi}} e^{-x^2} \left[1 + \frac{(2x^2)^2}{1 \cdot 3} + \frac{(2x^2)^4}{1 \cdot 3 \cdot 5} + \ldots \right]$$

Write a program based upon this series. Check the program by verifying a few of the numerical results given in the table of section 3.

4. Dawson's integral $F(x)$ is defined by the equation

$$F(x) = e^{-x^2} \int_0^x e^{t^2} dt$$

Obtain a series expansion and write a program to evaluate $F(x)$. The following results may be used to check the program:

x	1	2	5
F(x)	.53807 95069	.30134 03889	.10213 40744
	10		
	.05025 38471		

5. The complementary error function erfc x occurs in some applications. This is defined by the equation

$$\text{erfc } x = 1 - \text{erf } x$$

For large values of x it is not possible to evaluate erfc x by using the program of section 3 for erf x, because the value of erf x is practically indistinguishable from 1. Write a program to evaluate erfc x for large values of x by using the asymptotic expansion

$$\text{erfc } x = \frac{e^{-x^2}}{\sqrt{\pi} \, x} \left[1 - \frac{1}{(2x^2)} + \frac{1 \cdot 3}{(2x^2)^2} - \frac{1 \cdot 3 \cdot 5}{(2x^2)^3} + \ldots \right]$$

The following results may be used to check the program:

x	3.5	5	7
$x e^{x^2}$ erfc x	.5435276	.5535232	.5586004

10
.5614099

6. Show that

(a) $\displaystyle\int_0^b \frac{dx}{[(a^2 - x^2)(b^2 - x^2)]^{1/2}} = \frac{1}{a} K\left(\frac{b}{a}\right)$ $a > b \geq 0$

(b) $\displaystyle\int_0^b \frac{dx}{[(a^2 + x^2)(b^2 - x^2)]^{1/2}} = \frac{1}{\sqrt{a^2 + b^2}} K\left(\frac{b}{\sqrt{a^2 + b^2}}\right)$

$a \geq b \geq 0$

(c) $\displaystyle\int_0^\infty \frac{dx}{[(a^2 + x^2)(b^2 + x^2)]^{1/2}} = \frac{1}{a} K\left(\frac{\sqrt{a^2 - b^2}}{a}\right)$ $a \geq b > 0$

(d) $\displaystyle\int_b^a \frac{dx}{[(a^2 - x^2)(x^2 - b^2)]^{1/2}} = \frac{1}{a} K\left(\frac{\sqrt{a^2 - b^2}}{a}\right)$ $a \geq b > 0$

Evaluate the integrals numerically for a = .5 and b = .4.
Ans. (a) 3.99060 5555 (b) 2.76554 5985 (c,d) 3.50150 7606

7. Write a program to evaluate the Beta function B(p,q). The equation is

$$B(p,q) = \frac{\Gamma(p+q)}{\Gamma(p)\Gamma(q)} = \frac{(p+q-1)!}{(p-1)!(q-1)!}$$

8. The Struve function $H_v(x)$ is related to the Bessel function $J_v(x)$. For v = p = a positive integer or zero, the equation is

$$H_p(x) = \frac{\dfrac{2}{\pi}\left(\dfrac{x}{2}\right)^{p+1}}{\dfrac{1}{2}\dfrac{3}{2}\dfrac{5}{2} \cdots \cdots \left(p+\dfrac{1}{2}\right)} \left[1 - \frac{\left(\dfrac{x}{2}\right)^2}{\dfrac{3}{2}\left(p+\dfrac{3}{2}\right)} + \frac{\left(\dfrac{x}{2}\right)^4}{\dfrac{3}{2}\dfrac{5}{2}\left(p+\dfrac{3}{2}\right)\left(p+\dfrac{5}{2}\right)} - \cdots \cdots \right]$$

Write a program to evaluate the Struve function $H_p(x)$. The following numerical values of $H_p(x)$ may be used to check the program:

p \ x	1	2	3	5
0	.56865 66	.79085 88	.57430 61	−.18521 68
1	.19845 73	.64676 37	1.02010 96	.80781 19

4

NUMERICAL INTEGRATION

The problem of evaluating a definite integral occurs frequently in applications. The best procedure is to find an exact analytical solution. However, this is often impossible. A second method is to expand the integrand into an infinite series and integrate term by term. We have used this procedure in chapter 3. A third method is to calculate the value of the integrand at a number of discrete points and replace the integral by a weighted sum, i.e. approximate the value of the integral by an equation of the type

$$\int_a^b f(x)dx = (b - a) \sum w_i f(x_i) \tag{1}$$

where w_i is an appropriate weighting factor. In this chapter we shall consider several methods of this type. It will be assumed throughout the first three sections that the integrand is continuous and the interval is finite.

1. Simpson's rule

One very simple and widely used formula for numerical integration is

$$I = \int_{x_0}^{x_2} ydx = \frac{h}{3}(y_0 + 4y_1 + y_2) \tag{2}$$

Points 0 and 2 are the end points and point 1 is the midpoint of the interval; as shown in Fig. 1; h is the length of one subinterval. Equation (2) can be derived by passing a parabola through the three points. This formula is exact if $y = f(x)$ is a polynomial of degree ≤ 3. In general it is an approximation. Better accuracy is obtained by breaking the interval into an even number n of subintervals each of length h

FIGURE 1

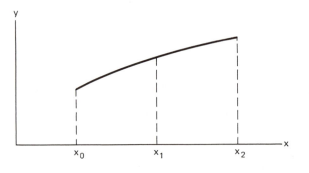

as shown in Fig. 2 and applying equation (2) to successive pairs of subintervals. This leads to

$$I = \int_{x_0}^{x_n} y\,dx = \frac{h}{3}(y_0 + 4y_1 + 2y_2 + 4y_3 + 2y_4 + \ldots + y_n) \quad (3)$$

or

$$I = \frac{h}{3}\left[(y_0 + y_n) + \sum_{i=1}^{n-1} w_i y_i\right] \qquad w_i = 2 \text{ or } 4 \qquad (4)$$

Equations (2), (3), and (4) are known as Simpson's rule.

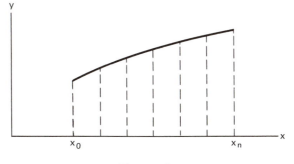

FIGURE 2

The program appears below. The first three lines assign the labels A, B, and C to the input parameters x_0, x_n, and n, respectively. Line 3 also calculates h, the length of the subinterval. Lines 4 and 5 calculate y_n and y_0, respectively. These are inserted into the partial sum in data register 07. Line 6 deducts 1 from the number n stored in data register 03. This will be used as a counter in a Dsz loop for the $n - 1$ intermediate points. Line 7 stores the weighting factor $w_i = 4$. Line 8 is the first line of the Dsz loop. It calculates $w_i y_i$ and adds it to the partial sum. Line 9 switches the coefficient w_i from 4 to 2 (or vice versa) in preparation for the next cycle. Line 10 executes the loop. Line 11 completes the evaluation of the integral. Line 12 is the function subroutine for the integral

$$I = \int_0^{\pi/2} x^2 \cos x\,dx \qquad (5)$$

```
0   LRN                          000

1   2nd Lbl A   ST001   R/S       005
```

2 2nd Lbl B   STO02   R/S   010

3 2nd Lbl C   STO03 $\frac{1}{x}$ × (RCL02 − RCL01)

    = STO04   026

4 RCL02   STO05   SBR082   STO07   035

5 RCL01   STO05   SBR082   SUM07   044

6 2nd Op 33   046

7 4 STO06   049

8 RCL04   SUM05   SBR082 × RCL06 = SUM07   062

9 6 − RCL06 = STO06   069

10 2nd Dsz 3049   073

11 RCL04 × RCL07 ÷ 3 = R/S   082

12 2nd Rad   RCL05 x^2 × RCL05 2nd cos = INV SBR   092

    LRN

Contents of data registers

01 x_0 02 x_n 03 $n - i$ 04 h   05 x_i 06 w_i = 2 or 4

07 partial sum $\Sigma\ w_i y_i$

The input/output operation is

Press x_0 A x_n B   n C

Display   I

The usual procedure in using Simpson's rule is to make several approximations with different values of n. It is not necessary to punch in the full input for approximations after the first. The values of x_0

and x_n remain in the calculator from the original input. Results after the first are obtained by pressing n C.

The accurate value of the integral (5) is

$$I = \frac{\pi^2}{4} - 2 = .4674011003$$

Numerical results from the program are given below.

n	2	4	8	16	32
I	.4568	.46689	.467371	.4673993	.46740099

The first eleven lines of the program are general; only the subroutine in the last line is concerned with the specific function. As a result the same program can be applied to other integrals. Only the function subroutine must be rewritten in each case. With the program still in the calculator, we press GTO082 LRN, followed by the new subroutine and another LRN statement. Consider

$$I = \int_0^1 \frac{\ln(1 + x)}{1 + x^2} \, dx \qquad (6)$$

The last line of the program now becomes

12   RCL05 + 1 = ln x ÷ (RCL05 x^2 + 1) = INV SBR   098

The accurate value of the integral is

$$I = \frac{\pi}{8} \ln 2 = .2721982613$$

Numerical results from the program are given in the following table.

n	2	4	8	16	32
I	.2740	.27233	.272206	.2721987	.27219829

In the foregoing two examples the accuracy of the results could be checked by comparing them with exact solutions. This is not possible in a practical problem—if an exact solution is known, there is no point in a numerical evaluation. The accuracy of an evaluation is inferred by comparing two results with different values of n. The results may be assumed to be correct up to the point through which the digits coincide. It follows from the last two results that the value of the desired integral is .272198.

Several difficulties sometimes occur in using Simpson's rule, and we shall now consider the most common ones. Even when the integrand is continuous, it may have indeterminacies at one or more points, most often at an end. Consider, for example

$$I = \int_0^2 \frac{\sin x}{x} \, dx \tag{7}$$

At the point $x = 0$, the integrand has the form $0/0$. It is easily found by l'Hopital's rule that its value at this point is 1, but this evaluation cannot be made by the program; it must be inserted. We therefore revise line 5 of the program as shown below.

5   RCL01   ST005   1 SUM07   2nd Nop   2nd Nop   044

The revised line 5 contains only 7 operational steps instead of 9. Instead of rewriting the entire program with new transfer numbers, it is advantageous to use the no-operation key as shown. This fills two program spaces with null statements. The location numbers of the subsequent statements then remain unchanged. Also, the function subroutine of line 12 becomes

12   2nd Rad   RCL05 2nd sin ÷ RCL05 = INV SBR   091

The accurate value of the integral is 1.6054129768. The program gives the approximations listed below.

n	2	4	8	16
I	1.6069	1.60550	1.605418	1.6054133
	32			
	1.60541300			

Some care must be taken in using Simpson's rule when the integrand is very large in a small part of the interval and negligible elsewhere, such as a rapidly varying exponential. In this case a uniform spacing of points over the entire interval cannot be expected to give good results. The points must be spaced more closely in the region in which the integrand is large.

The basic Simpson's rule is unsuitable for a function which contains an oscillatory component. In this case the points must be spaced closely enough so that the subinterval h is a small fraction not merely of the interval, but of the wave length. If the interval contains a number of waves, the required number of points is so great that the method becomes impractical. A modification of Simpson's rule has been developed by Filon for the integrals

$$\int_{x_0}^{x_n} f(x) \sin x \, dx \qquad \int_{x_0}^{x_n} f(x) \cos x \, dx \qquad (8a,b)$$

where $f(x)$ is a function of the type which could be integrated directly by the ordinary Simpson's rule. The method is described in reference 8. The formulas can also be found in reference 3, pages 890–891.

2. Gauss integration

The basic principle of numerical integration is to replace an integral by a weighted sum. Simpson's rule consists of repeated applications of the parabolic formula (2). There are more efficient methods of utilizing data from a large number of points. One procedure is to again use equally spaced points, but fit a higher order polynominal to all of the points. Formulas obtained in this way are known as Newton-Cotes formulas. However, it is more efficient to drop the requirement of equally spaced points, which is entirely arbitrary. This doubles the number of adjustable parameters in equation (1), since the x_i's may now be chosen for optimum computational efficiency as well as the w_i's. In this way it is possible to fit a polynomial of order $2n - 1$ to n points. This procedure is known as Gauss integration. The derivation, which can be found in section 1 of the appendix, is rather lengthy. However, the results are simple and easy to use. The basic formula for Gauss integration is

$$I = \int_a^b f(x) \, dx = \frac{b-a}{2} \sum_{i=1}^{n} w_i f(x_i) \qquad (9a)$$

where w_i is a weighting factor and

$$x_i = \frac{b+a}{2} + \frac{b-a}{2} \xi_i \qquad (9b)$$

The parameter n is the number of points (not the number of subintervals). The points are symmetrically located, as shown in Fig. 3 for $n = 8$. The end points are not included in the set of points at which the function is to be evaluated. (It is for this reason that the limits in equation (9a) are denoted as a and b instead of x_1 and x_n). It is convenient to choose an even number of points and arrange them in symmetrically located pairs. Then the formulas become

$$I = \frac{b-a}{2} \sum_{i=1}^{n/2} w_i \left[f(\bar{x}_i) + f(\tilde{x}_i) \right] \tag{10a}$$

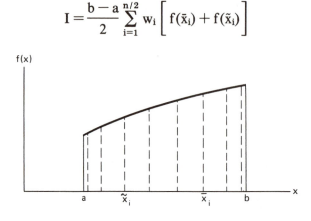

FIGURE 3

$$\bar{x}_i = \frac{b+a}{2} + \frac{b-a}{2} \xi_i \qquad \tilde{x}_i = \frac{b+a}{2} - \frac{b-a}{2} \xi_i \tag{10b,c}$$

The parameters ξ_i and w_i are found from the following table, which is abstracted from reference 3. (The same results can be obtained from a program in section 1 of the appendix.) Extensive formulas and tables for various forms of Gauss integration can be found in references 3 and 9.

n	ξ_i	w_i	n	ξ_i	w_i
2	0.57735 02692	1.00000 00000		0.18343 46425	0.36268 37834
				.52553 24099	.31370 66459
4	.33998 10436	.65214 51549	8	.79666 64774	.22238 10345
	.86113 63116	.34785 48451		.96028 98565	.10122 85363
6	.23861 91861	.46791 39346			
	.66120 93865	.36076 15730			
	.93246 95142	.17132 44924			

A program based upon equations (10) follows. Line 1 divides the parameter n by 2 and stores the result in data register 04. This is used as a counter in a Dsz loop. There are n/2 cycles, and each cycle carries out the calculation for two symmetrically located points. There is a slight difficulty in setting up a Dsz loop for this problem because the ξ_i's and w_i's are not given by formulas; they must be obtained from a table such as the one above. We use the scheme of chapter 1, section 6. The ξ_i's and w_i's are punched into the calculator with the numerical input and transferred into the program by indirect addressing. Line 2 adds 9 to the counter in data register 04; it will then serve as an index for indirect addressing of the ξ_i's, which are stored in data registers 10, 11, ... Lines 3 and 4 calculate $\bar{x}_i$. Line 5 adds another 10 to the counter in data register 04; it will then serve as an index for indirect addressing of the w_i's, which are stored in data registers 20, 21, ... Line 6 calculates $w_i f(\bar{x}_i)$ and adds it to the partial sum. Line 7 calculates $\bar{x}_i$. Line 8 calculates $w_i f(\bar{x}_i)$ and adds it to the partial sum. Line 9 subtracts 19 from the counter in data register 04, so that it is ready to serve as a counter for the Dsz loop. Line 10 executes the loop, and line 11 completes the evaluation of I. Line 12 is the function subroutine for the integral (5)

$$I = \int_0^{\pi/2} x^2 \cos x \, dx$$

that has been evaluated previously by Simpson's rule. The program can accommodate data for as many as 20 points — 10 ξ_i's in data registers 10 through 19 and 10 w_i's in data registers 20 through 29. The program is entirely general with the exception of the function subroutine in the last line.

0	LRN	000
1	RCL03 ÷ 2 = STO04 0 STO06	010
2	9 SUM04	013
3	RCL02 − RCL01 = × RCL 2nd Ind 04	022
4	+ RCL02 + RCL01 = ÷ 2 = STO05	034
5	10 SUM04	038
6	SBR089 × RCL 2nd Ind 04 = SUM06	047
7	RCL02 + RCL01 − RCL05 = STO05	058

8   SBR089 × RCL 2nd Ind 04 = SUM06   067

9   19 INV SUM04   072

10 2nd Dsz 4010   076

11 RCL02 − RCL01 = × RCL06 ÷ 2 = R/S   089

12 2nd Rad RCL05 x² × RCL05 2nd cos = INV SBR   099

    LRN

Contents of data registers

01 a   02 b   03 n   04 $i = \frac{n}{2}, \frac{n}{2} - 1, \ldots, 1$ 05 x_i

06 partial sum $\Sigma\, w_i f(x_i)$ 10 ξ_1 11 $\xi_2 \ldots$ 20 w_1 21 $w_2 \ldots$

The detailed input/output for $n = 8$ is

Press   a STO01   b STO02   8 STO03
        .1834346425 STO010   .3626837834 STO020
        .5255324099 STO011   .3137066459 STO021
        .7966664774 STO012   .2223810345 STO022
        .9602898565 STO013   .1012285363 STO023
        RST   R/S

Display   I

For the integral (5), the program gives the result $I = .4674011003$. This agrees with the exact value to the full extent of the calculator display.

We again consider the integral (6)

$$I = \int_0^1 \frac{\ln(1+x)}{1+x^2}\, dx$$

which has been evaluated previously by Simpson's rule. The last line of the program now becomes

12   RCL05 + 1 = ln x ÷ (RCL05 x² + 1) = INV SBR   105

The numerical result is I = .2721982613, which again agrees with the exact value to the full extent of the calculator display.

The two foregoing examples may tend to give a false sense of confidence in the accuracy of Gauss integration. This method sometimes gives rather poor results, even for some very simple integrals. Consider

$$I = \int_0^1 \sqrt{x}\, dx \qquad (11)$$

The function subroutine now becomes

12 RCL05 $\sqrt{x}$ INV SBR   093

The correct result is 0.6666. . . . , but the program with n = 8 gives 0.6683. . . . The present result is much poorer than the two preceding ones. This situation will be clarified to some extent later in this section. However, there is no reliable way to determine the accuracy of Gauss integration in advance. It is always necessary to carry out at least two evaluations of an integral using different values of n. The results may be assumed to be correct up to the point through which the digits coincide.

The restrictions noted for Simpson's rule at the end of section 1 also apply to Gauss integration. However, indeterminacies are less likely to occur with Gauss integration than with Simpson's rule, because the former method does not use the end points.

It is desirable at this point to briefly consider the relative merits of Simpson's rule and Gauss integration. Simpson's rule is expressed by a program which is simple and easy to use, but the running time is often undesirably long because the process is not very efficient. Gauss integration is more efficient and the program is faster for a given level of accuracy, but a set of ten digit numerical constants

FIGURE 4

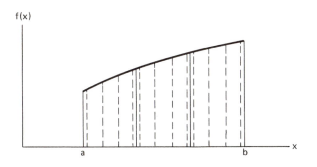

must be punched into the calculator each time the program is used. Each calculation with a new value of n requires a completely new set of constants. Also, this must always be done at least twice because two independent calculations are necessary to verify the accuracy of a result, and it often has to be done several times. It is often more convenient to use the modified form of Gauss integration that is shown schematically in Fig. 4. In this method the interval is broken into m equal panels. The Gauss method with n points is then applied to each panel, and the results for the m panels are added. Fig. 4 shows the scheme for m = 3, n = 4. This method is less accurate than a direct application of the Gauss method with mn points, but it reduces the tabular imput to n entries instead of mn. Also, the input only has to be inserted once. Different levels of accuracy are obtained by varying m while keeping n fixed. This method represents a compromise between speed of operation and simplicity of input. The equations are

$$I = \frac{h}{2} \sum_{j=0}^{m-1} \sum_{i=1}^{n/2} w_i [f(\bar{x}_i) + f(\tilde{x}_i)] \tag{12a}$$

$$h = \frac{b - a}{m} \tag{12b}$$

$$x_j = a + jh \qquad j = 0,1,2, \ldots, m - 1 \tag{12c}$$

$$\bar{x}_i = x_j + \frac{h}{2}(1 + \xi_i) \qquad \tilde{x}_i = x_j + \frac{h}{2}(1 - \xi_i) \tag{12d,e}$$

The program that follows is straightforward. It consists essentially of a double loop. The inner loop, which runs from line 4 through line 11, is equivalent to the basic Gauss program given earlier. This calculates the required summation for each panel. The outer loop, which runs from line 3 through line 13, moves the execution from panel to panel and adds the results. Line 14 completes the evaluation of I and line 15 is the function subroutine for the integral (5).

```
0   LRN                                                      000


1   STO04 1/x × (RCL02 − RCL01) = STO07   0 STO006    017


2   RCL01   STO09                                      021
```

3 RCL03 ÷ 2 = STO08   028

4 9 SUM08   031

5 RCL 2nd Ind 08 + 1 = × RCL07 ÷ 2 + RCL09 =
   STO05   047

6 10 SUM08   051

7 SBR109 × RCL 2nd Ind 08 = SUM06   060

8 2 × RCL09 + RCL07 − RCL05 = STO05   073

9 SBR109 × RCL 2nd Ind 08 = SUM06   082

10 19 INV SUM08   087

11 2nd Dsz 8028   091

12 RCL07 SUM09   095

13 2nd Dsz 4021   099

14 RCL06 × RCL07 ÷ 2 = R/S RST   109

15 2nd Rad RCL05 x^2 × RCL05 2nd cos = INV SBR   119

    LRN

Contents of data registers

01 a   02 b   03 n   04 m − j   05 x_i 06 partial sum $\Sigma\, w_i\, f(x_i)$
07 h   08 i $= \dfrac{n}{2}, \dfrac{n}{2} - 1, \ldots, 1$ 09 x_j 10 ξ_1 11 $\xi_2 \ldots$
20 w_1 21 $w_2 \ldots$

The detailed input/output operation is exactly the same as that of the original Gauss program, with one addition—the value of m is pressed immediately before pressing RST R/S. The program is organized so that the values of a, b, and n remain in the original data registers throughout the calculation. The initial calculation is ordinarily made with m = 1. More accurate approximations are then made with higher values of m. The input for each subsequent value of m is simply m R/S. For the integral (5) with n = 8 and m = 1, we again obtain the accurate result I = .4674011003.

We have already observed that the convergence of the Gauss process varies greatly between different integrals. In many cases it is excellent, but in other cases such as (11)

$$I = \int_0^1 \sqrt{x}\, dx$$

we have seen that it is relatively poor. The difficulty of using the Gauss method with a large number of points is partially alleviated by the modified program, but it is still highly desirable to have an efficient process if possible. Sometimes an integral can be converted into an improved form by a simple substitution; for example, by writing x^2 for x in the foregoing integral, we obtain the alternate form

$$I = 2 \int_0^1 x^2\, dx$$

that is well suited to Gauss integration.

Some light can be thrown on this problem by considering the integral

$$I = \int_0^1 \frac{\text{arc sin } x}{x}\, dx \tag{13}$$

The exact value is

$$I = \frac{\pi}{2} \ln 2 = 1.088793045$$

We evaluate the integral as it stands by using the modified Gauss program. The function subroutine is

```
15   2nd Rad   RCL05   INV 2nd sin ÷ RCL05 =
     INV SBR                                          119
```

With n = 8 and several values of m, we obtain the following results

m	1	2	3	4
I	1.08856	1.08871	1.088747	1.088763

5
1.088772

These results are good enough for many practical applications, but there is an error which diminishes rather slowly as m increases. Also, the running time is undesirably long for large values of m.

The Gauss method is based upon the approximation of the exact function by a polynomial. The method works well if the function can be represented throughout the interval by a Taylor series which is substantially convergent for terms of order no higher than those contained in the approximating polynomial. The best results will be obtained if the integrand is represented by a rapidly convergent Taylor series. The difficulty with the integral (13) is due to the presence of the arc sine term, which has a very slowly convergent Taylor expansion. The efficiency of the numerical evaluation can be enhanced by getting rid of this term. At the same time we must be careful not to introduce a singularity. The best procedure is to write sin x for x. Then the integral becomes

$$I = \int_0^{\pi/2} \frac{x}{\tan x} \, dx$$

The function subroutine for the modified Gauss program is

15 2nd Rad   RCL05 ÷ 2nd tan = INV SBR   116

With n = 8 and m = 1 we find that I = 1.088793045, which is correct to the full extent of the calculator display.

A similar example is provided by the integral

$$I = \int_0^{\pi/2} \sin x \, \ln \sin x \, dx \qquad (14)$$

that has the exact value

$$I = \ln 2 - 1 = -.3068528194$$

We evaluate the integral as it stands by using the modified Gauss program. The function subroutine is

15 2nd Rad   RCL05 2nd sin × ln x = INV SBR   117

With n = 8 and several values of m, we obtain the results

m	1	2	3	4	5
−I	.306973	.306883	.306866	.306860	.3068576

The results are adequate, but there is room for improvement. In this case the convergence is retarded by the presence of the ln sin x factor in the integrand, since the interval contains the origin. The best way to remove this factor is to integrate by parts. Then we find that

$$I = [(1 - \cos x) \ln \sin x]_0^{\pi/2} - \int_0^{\pi/2} (1 - \cos x) \cot x \, dx$$

$$= -\int_0^{\pi/2} \frac{1 - \cos x}{\tan x} \, dx$$

The function subroutine is

    15   2nd Rad   RCL05 2nd cos − 1 = ÷ RCL05 2nd tan =
         INV SBR   122

With n = 8 and m = 1 we obtain the result I = −.3068528194, which is correct to the full extent of the calculator display.

3. Romberg integration

We have considered Simpson's rule and Gauss integration. Another widely used method of evaluating definite integrals numerically is Romberg integration. This method is more efficient than Simpson's rule. It is less efficient than Gauss integration, but it is sometimes preferred because it requires no tabular input. Romberg integration consists of an extrapolation process which starts with the trapezoidal rule. This is

$$\int_a^b f(x) \, dx = \frac{l}{2n} \left[f(a) + 2f\left(a + \frac{l}{n}\right) + 2f\left(a + \frac{2l}{n}\right) + \dots + f(b) \right] \quad (15)$$

where $l = b - a$, the length of the interval, and n is the number of equal subintervals. We consider the sequence of approximations obtained by setting $n = 1, 2, 4, 8, \ldots, 2^k, \ldots$. The first few values of I_k are

$$I_0 = \frac{l}{2}[f(a) + f(b)] \tag{16}$$

$$I_1 = \frac{l}{4}\left[f(a) + 2f\left(a + \frac{l}{2}\right) + f(b)\right]$$

$$I_2 = \frac{l}{8}\left[f(a) + 2f\left(a + \frac{l}{4}\right) + 2f\left(a + \frac{l}{2}\right) + 2f\left(a + \frac{3l}{4}\right) + f(b)\right]$$

It is not necessary to calculate values of f for all of the points in each approximation. Only the odd points in each approximation are new. Thus we write

$$I_1 = \frac{I_0}{2} + \frac{l}{2}f\left(a + \frac{l}{2}\right)$$

$$I_2 = \frac{I_1}{2} + \frac{l}{4}\left[f\left(a + \frac{l}{4}\right) + f\left(a + \frac{3l}{4}\right)\right]$$

In general

$$I_k = \frac{I_{k-1}}{2} + \frac{l}{2^k}\sum_{i=1,3,5}^{2^k-1} f\left(a + \frac{il}{2^k}\right)$$

$$= \frac{I_{k-1}}{2} + \frac{l}{2^k}\sum_{i=1}^{2^{k-1}} f\left(a + \frac{2i-1}{2^k}l\right) \tag{17}$$

The Romberg method consists of developing an array of approximations $I_{k,j}$ as shown in the table below. The elements in the first column are the results I_k found from the trapezoidal rule. We now denote these as $I_{k,1}$. The remaining elements are found by repeated applications of the formula

$$I_{k,j+1} = \frac{4^j I_{k+1,j} - I_{k,j}}{4^j - 1} \tag{18}$$

The results in the first row converge toward the exact value. The theory of Romberg integration can be found in references 10 and 11.

k $\searrow$ j	1	2	3	4
0	$I_{0,1}$ $\rightarrow$	$I_{0,2}$ $\rightarrow$	$I_{0,3}$ $\rightarrow$	$I_{0,4}$
	$\downarrow$ $\nearrow$	$\nearrow$	$\nearrow$	(15)
1	$I_{1,1}$	$I_{1,2}$	$I_{1,3}$	
	$\bot$ $\nearrow$	$\nearrow$	(14)	
2	$I_{2,1}$	$I_{2,2}$		
	$\downarrow$ $\nearrow$	(13)		
3	$I_{3,1}$			
	(12)			

The program appears below. The first time the program is run, it executes lines 1 through 5. Line 1 stores the appropriate value of a. Line 2 stores b, calculates and stores l, and stores the starting values K = 0 and n = 1. Lines 3 through 5 use equation (16) to calculate $I_0 = I_{0,1}$.

Subsequent cycles start with line 6. Lines 6 through 9 use equation (17) to calculate an element $I_k = I_{k,1}$ in the first column of the Romberg table, starting with $I_1 = I_{1,1}$ in the second cycle. Line 6 adjusts the values of k and n for the new cycle and clears data register 10, which will contain the summation in equation (17). Lines 7 and 8 constitute a Dsz loop which calculates the f's and adds them to obtain the summation in equation (17). Line 9 completes the evaluation of $I_{k,1}$, which is an element of the first column of the Romberg table.

Lines 10 through 13 use equation (18) to generate the elements along a diagonal of the Romberg table. Equation (18) is a recurrence relation, but it is more complicated than the recurrence relations considered in chapter 1, section 5. There are two subscripts instead of one, and the equation generates the two dimensional Romberg array instead of a one dimensional array of the type considered in chapter 1. Line 10 stores the appropriate starting values of k and j in data registers 00 and 08, respectively. It also stores the parameter j + 11 in data register 09 and brings $I_{k,1}$ into the display register to start the Dsz loop of lines 11 and 12. The parameter in data register 09 is used as an index for indirect addressing in the Dsz loop, which executes equation (18). Line 13 stores and displays the final result, which appears as an element in the first row of the Romberg table.

Line 14 is the function subroutine for the integral (10), which is

$$I = \int_0^{\pi/2} x^2 \cos x \, dx$$

At the three places in the program where the subroutine statement appears, it is immediately preceded by the value of x_i. Therefore it is not necessary to store x_i in the main program. In the present example it is not necessary to store it anywhere. With a more complicated integrand, it may be necessary to store x_i in the subroutine. This can be accomplished by writing STO05 at the beginning of the subroutine.

0	LRN	000
1	2nd Lbl A STO01 R/S	005
2	2nd Lbl B STO02 − RCL01 = STO03 0 STO04 1 STO06	021
3	RCL01 SBR149 STO10	028
4	RCL02 SBR149 SUM10	035
5	RCL10 × RCL03 ÷ 2 = STO11 STO12 R/S	048
6	2nd Op 24 RCL06 STO07 2 2nd Prd06 0 STO10	060
7	2 × RCL07 − 1 = ÷ RCL06 × RCL03 + RCL01 = SBR149 SUM10	082
8	2nd Dsz 7060	086
9	2 Inv 2nd Prd11 RCL10 × RCL03 ÷ RCL06 = SUM11	101
10	RCL04 STO00 1 STO08 12 STO09 RCL11	114
11	2nd Exc 2nd Ind09 − 4y^x RCL08 × RCL 2nd Ind09 =	125
12	÷ (1 − 4y^x RCL08) = 2nd Op 28 2nd Op 29 2nd Dsz 0114	143
13	STO 2nd Ind09 R/S GTO048	149
14	2nd Rad x^2 × $\sqrt{x}$ 2nd cos = INV SBR	156
	LRN	

Contents of data registers

00 k, k − 1, ... , 1   01 a   02 b   03 l 04 k   05 x_i^*
06 n = 2^k 07 i = $\frac{n}{2}, \frac{n}{2} - 1$, ... , 1   08 j = 1,2,3, ...
09 j + 11   10 partial sum in equation (17)   11,12 $I_{k,1}$
13 $I_{k-1,2}$ 14 $I_{k-2,3}$

Input/output

Press   a A   b B   R/S   R/S

Display $I_{0,1}$ $I_{0,2}$ $I_{0,3}$

An overall review of the operation of the program may be desirable. We have already observed that in the first cycle, the program executes lines 1 through 5. The result is $I_{0,1}$, the element in the upper left corner of the Romberg table. Each subsequent cycle is activated by pressing the R/S key. Each cycle calculates the next element of the first column of the table in lines 6 through 9 and then generates the diagonal elements in lines 10 through 13. The results are stored as they are found, overwriting the elements of the preceding diagonal. The data registers are indicated in the table. Only the last result of each cycle, which appears in the first row of the table, is displayed automatically. However, an entire diagonal can be recalled by pressing RCL12, RCL13, ...

The Romberg table for the integral (5) appears below. The numbers in the first column are the results of the trapezoidal rule. The numbers in the second column correspond to Simpson's rule with the index k shifted by 1. This can be deduced from equation (18) and verified by referring back to section 1. It can be seen that the

k \ j	1	2	3	4	5
0	.00000	.4567656	.46756523	.467400757	.4674011004
1	.34257	.4668903	.46740333	.467401099	
2	.43581	.4673713	.46740113		
3	.45948	.4673993			
4	.46542				

* Not stored in the present example.

final results in the first row converge toward the exact result more rapidly than the Simpson results and much more rapidly than the trapezoidal results. The last result is correct to the full extent of the calculator display, with the exception of a slight discrepancy in the last digit.

It is proved in reference 10 that the Romberg process converges toward the exact result. However, it does not always converge rapidly. The integrals of section 2 that showed poor convergence with Gauss integration converge even more poorly with Romberg integration. Some other examples of slow convergence are given in reference 10. The convergence of the Romberg process is sometimes slower than that of Simpson's rule or even the trapezoidal rule. The safest procedure in using Romberg integration is to print the entire table. The convergence of the various processes can then be examined and the most satisfactory result can be chosen.

Since the Romberg process uses the end points, indeterminacies sometimes occur. Consider the integral (13) of section 2, which is rewritten below

$$I = \int_0^1 \frac{\arcsin x}{x} \, dx$$

The integrand is indeterminate at the point $x = 0$, but the correct limit is clearly 1. The procedure is similar to that given in section 1 for Simpson's rule. Instead of rewriting the entire program, we revise line 3 to read

3   1.000   STO10   028

There are three functional steps in the new line 3: 1 STO10. We have added four nonfunctional steps by inserting a decimal point and three zeros in order to make the length of the new line match that of the original. (The Nop statement could also have been used.) The function subroutine of line 14 becomes

14   2nd Rad   ÷ INV 2nd sin $= \frac{1}{x}$ INV SBR   156

The correct value of the integral is $\pi \ln 2/2 = 1.088793$. Results given by the program appear in the table below. For this problem the Romberg method has little merit; the Romberg results in the first row are not significantly better than the Simpson results in the second column.

k \ j	1	2	3	4	5	6
0	1.2854	1.1266	1.1010	1.0930	1.0903	1.0893
1	1.1663	1.1026	1.0932	1.0903	1.0893	
2	1.1185	1.0938	1.0904	1.0893		
3	1.0999	1.0906	1.0893			
4	1.0929	1.0894				
5	1.0903					

Like the Gauss method, the Romberg method is sensitive to the form of the integrand. As in section 2, we now consider the equivalent integral

$$I = \int_0^{\pi/2} \frac{x}{\tan x}\, dx$$

which is obtained by writing sin x for x in (13). The integrand is indeterminate at the lower limit, and the factor tan x is infinite at the upper limit. Lines 3 and 4 of the program are revised to

3   1.000   ST010   028

4   0.000   SUM10   035

The function subroutine becomes

14   2nd Rad ÷ 2nd tan = INV SBR   154

Numerical results appear in the table below. It can be seen that these results are much better than those obtained from the original integral (13). The Simpson results in the second column are also greatly improved, although to a lesser extent than the Romberg results.

k \ j	1	2	3	4
0	.7854	1.084266	1.088704	1.088792
1	1.0095	1.088427	1.088791	
2	1.0687	1.088768		
3	1.0838			

4. Integrals with discontinuous integrands

The methods which we have considered in the first three sections apply only to proper integrals. The integrands are continuous and the intervals are finite. In this section the intervals are still finite, but the integrands are infinite at one or both end points. Simpson's rule breaks down for an integral of this type, since y_0 or y_n or both are infinite. It is possible to obtain a numerical result by applying Gauss integration directly, since the end points do not appear explicitly in the formulas, but this procedure is unsound and does not usually lead to good results. The best procedure is to transform the improper integral into a proper integral, then use a method from one of the first three sections. We shall consider three commonly used methods of removing a singularity in the integrand.

One useful method is substitution. We illustrate this with the integral

$$I = \int_0^{2.25} \frac{e^{-x}}{\sqrt{x}}\, dx \tag{19}$$

which has an infinite integrand at the lower limit. We write x^2 for x. Then

$$I = 2 \int_0^{1.5} e^{-x^2}\, dx$$

This is a proper integral. We use the modified Gauss program of section 2. The function subroutine for the new integral is

$$15 \quad \text{RCL05} \ x^2 \ \text{INV} \ \ln x \ \frac{1}{x} \quad \text{INV SBR} \qquad 116$$

With $n = 8$ and $m = 1$, the numerical result is $I = 1.712376787$, which is accurate to the full extent of the calculator display.*

A second method is integration by parts. An example is provided by the integral

$$I = \int_0^1 \frac{\ln x}{1 + x^2}\, dx \tag{20}$$

* This can easily be verified by using the program of chapter 3, section 3.

that has a logarithmic singularity at the lower limit. We find that

$$I = [\ln x \text{ arc tan } x]_0^1 - \int_0^1 \frac{\text{arc tan } x}{x} dx$$

$$= -\int_0^1 \frac{\text{arc tan } x}{x} dx$$

The new integral is proper, and it can be evaluated numerically as it stands. However, it is somewhat similar to the integral (13), and it leads to a rather inefficient numerical process because of the arc tangent factor. It is desirable to transform the integral further by writing tan x for x. Then we have

$$I = -\int_0^{\pi/4} \frac{x}{\sin x \cos x} dx = -\frac{1}{2}\int_0^{\pi/2} \frac{x}{\sin x} dx$$

We use the modified Gauss program. The function subroutine for the last integral on the right is

15   2nd Rad   RCL05 ÷ 2nd sin = INV SBR   116

With n = 8 and m = 1 we find that I = −.9159655943, which is correct to the full extent of the calculator display.

A third method of eliminating a singularity is to add and subtract a related integral. We again use the integral (20) as an example. We rewrite it as

$$I = \int_0^1 \ln x \, dx - \int_0^1 \left(\ln x - \frac{\ln x}{1 + x^2} \right) dx$$

$$= -1 - \int_0^1 \frac{x^2 \ln x}{1 + x^2} dx$$

The new integral is proper; the integrand is equal to zero at the lower limit. We apply the modified Gauss program. The function subroutine is

15   RCL05 x² × RCL05ln x ÷ (RCL05 x² + 1)
      = INV SBR   126

With n = 8 and several values of m, we obtain the following results

m	1	2	3	4
$-I$	.9159667	.91596571	.91596563	.91596561

5
.915965602

Some further examples may be of interest. Consider

$$I = \int_0^1 \frac{\ln x}{\sqrt{1-x}} \, dx \tag{21}$$

The integrand is infinite at the lower limit. (It is zero at the upper limit.) We write $\sin^2 x$ for x. Then it follows that

$$I = 4 \int_0^{\pi/2} \sin x \ln \sin x \, dx$$

which is proper. The new integral is identical to (14), which has already been evaluated. The result is $I = -1.227411278$.

This procedure can be made more general. An integral of the type

$$I = \int_a^b \frac{f(x)}{\sqrt{b-x}} \, dx \tag{22}$$

can often be evaluated by writing $b \sin^2 x$ for x. This usually leads to a successful result when $f(x)$ is a continuous function, and sometimes succeeds even when it is not, as in the preceding example.

It is not always easy to see by inspection what procedure will lead to a satisfactory result; sometimes it may be necessary to try two or more methods or a combination of methods. The integral

$$I = \int_0^1 \frac{\ln x}{\sqrt{1-x^2}} \, dx \tag{23}$$

resembles the integral (21), and we might try to evaluate it by an analogous procedure, writing $\sin x$ for x. However, this does not work; the resulting integral still has a logarithmic singularity at the lower limit. Integration by parts leads to a more satisfactory result. Thus

$$I = [\ln x \, \text{arc} \sin x]_0^1 - \int_0^1 \frac{\text{arc} \sin x}{x} \, dx = -\int_0^1 \frac{\text{arc} \sin x}{x} \, dx$$

105

The new integral is identical to (13), which has already been evaluated. The result is $I = -1.088793045$.

There are special methods of the Gauss type for a number of integrals, both proper and improper. Some of these are more complicated than the basic Gauss method; others are simpler. One useful special method known as Gauss-Chebyshev integration evaluates integrals of the form

$$I = \int_a^b \frac{f(x)\, dx}{[(x - a)(b - x)]^{1/2}} \tag{24}$$

where $f(x)$ is a continuous function. (This can be evaluated by integration by parts followed by the standard Gauss integration, but the special method is simpler.) The formulas are

$$I = \frac{\pi}{n} \sum_{i=1}^{n} f(x_i) \tag{25a}$$

$$x_i = \frac{b + a}{2} + \frac{b - a}{2} \xi_i \tag{25b}$$

$$\xi_i = \cos \frac{(2i - 1)\pi}{2n} \tag{25c}$$

This method is much neater than the standard Gauss method. No tabular input is required because the ξ_i's are given by an explicit formula and there are no weighting factors. The program appears below; it is self-explanatory. The function subroutine in the last line is set up to evaluate the integral

$$I = \int_{-1}^{1} \frac{\cos x}{\sqrt{1 - x^2}}\, dx = 2 \int_{0}^{1} \frac{\cos x}{\sqrt{1 - x^2}}\, dx \tag{26}$$

0	LRN				000
1	2nd Lbl A	ST001	R/S		005
2	2nd Lbl B	ST002	R/S		010
3	2nd Lbl C	ST003	ST004	0 ST006 2nd Rad	020

4 $2 \times$ RCL04 $- 1 = \times$ 2nd $\pi \div 2 \div$ RCL03 $=$ 2nd cos   036

5 $\times$ (RCL02 $-$ RCL01) $+$ RCL02 $+$ RCL01 $= \div 2 =$ 054

6 SBR072   SUM06   059

7 2nd Dsz 4020   063

8 RCL06 $\times$ 2nd $\pi \div$ RCL03 $=$ R/S   072

9 2nd cos   INV SBR   074

   LRN

Contents of data registers

01 a   02 b   03 n   04 i $=$ n, n $-$ 1, n $-$ 2, ... , 1
05 x_i*   06 partial sum Σy_i

Input/output

Press   a A   b B   n C

Display   I

This program resembles the Romberg program of section 3 in one respect. In the example shown, it is not necessary to store x_i. With a more complicated integrand, it may be necessary to store x_i in the subroutine. This can be accomplished by writing STO05 at the beginning of the subroutine.

After a result has been found for one value of n, further approximations are obtained by pressing n C. With a $=$ $-$1, b $=$ 1, and several values of n, we obtain the results

n	2	3	4	5
I	2.388	2.4041	2.4039388	2.403939432
	6			
2.403939431				

The last result is accurate to the full extent of the calculator display.

* Not stored in the present example.

Other Gauss-Chebyshev algorithms are available for integrals of the type

$$\int_a^b \left(\frac{x-a}{b-x}\right)^{1/2} f(x)\,dx \quad \int_a^b [(x-a)(b-x)]^{1/2} f(x)\,dx \quad (27a,b)$$

where $f(x)$ is a continuous function. However, it is not necessary to write special programs for these. The program just given can be used by simply redefining $f(x)$ to include a factor of $(x-a)$ or $(x-a)(b-x)$. The integral (27b) can be evaluated directly by standard Gauss integration, since it is proper, but the special program is more efficient.

Formulas and tables for various types of Gauss integration can be found in references 9 and 3.

5. Integrals with infinite intervals

Integrals with infinite intervals are sometimes troublesome. Usually the best procedure for an integral of this type is a substitution. Consider

$$I = \int_0^\infty \frac{e^{-x}}{x^2+1}\,dx \tag{28}$$

the accurate value of which is .6214496242.* The easiest way to evaluate this integral is to write tan x for x. Then we have

$$I = \int_0^{\pi/2} e^{-\tan x}\,dx$$

which is proper. It is always possible to convert an infinite interval into a finite interval by the tangent substitution. However, it sometimes happens that the transformed integral has some new anomaly which causes as much trouble as the original one. In the present case there is no difficulty. We use the modified Gauss program. The function subroutine is

15   2nd RAD   RCL05   2nd tan INV ln x $\dfrac{1}{x}$ INV SBR   117

---

* Chapter 3, problem 1.

With n = 8 and several values of m, we obtain the results

m	1	2	3	4
I	.621479	.6214468	.6214499	.62144965

5
.621449605

Other substitutions can also be used. By writing $-\ln x$ for x, we obtain the integral

$$I = \int_0^1 \frac{dx}{(\ln x)^2 + 1}$$

However, this leads to a less efficient evaluation than the one just given.

An alternate procedure is to first break the interval and then make a substitution in one of the new integrals. Thus

$$I = \int_0^1 \frac{e^{-x}}{x^2 + 1} \, dx + \int_1^\infty \frac{e^{-x}}{x^2 + 1} \, dx \qquad (29)$$

By writing $1/x$ for x in the second integral, then combining the two integrals, we arrive at the result

$$I = \int_0^1 \frac{e^{-x} + e^{-1/x}}{x^2 + 1} \, dx$$

The function subroutine for the modified Gauss program is

15 RCL05 INV ln x $\frac{1}{x}$ + RCL05 $\frac{1}{x}$ INV ln x $\frac{1}{x}$ =

÷ (RCL05 x² + 1) = INV SBR   132

With n = 8 and several values of m, we obtain the results

m	1	2	3	4
I	.6214513	.62144989	.621449601	.621449625

5
.6214496242

Another procedure which is sometimes used as a last resort is to terminate the interval at some large but finite value of x, then apply numerical integration. Thus, for example, we can write

$$\int_0^\infty \frac{e^{-x}}{x^2+1} \, dx = \int_0^{10} \frac{e^{-x}}{x^2+1} \, dx + \int_{10}^\infty \frac{e^{-x}}{x^2+1} \, dx \qquad (30)$$

We discard the second integral on the right and apply the modified Gauss program to the first. The function subroutine is

$$15 \quad \text{RCL05 } x^2 + 1 = \frac{1}{x} \div \text{RCL05 INV ln } x = \text{INV SBR} \qquad 123$$

With n = 8 and several values of m, we obtain the results

m	1	2	3	4
I	.62103	.6214420	.6214455	.6214489

We take the final result as .621449, which is very close to the correct value. It is easy to check the error incurred by dropping the last term in equation (30). We observe that

$$\int_{10}^\infty \frac{e^{-x}}{x^2+1} \, dx < \frac{1}{101} \int_{10}^\infty e^{-x} dx = \frac{1}{101 \cdot e^{10}} = .00000045$$

There are two special methods of the Gauss type for the evaluation of integrals with infinite invervals. Unfortunately their utility is limited. An integral of the type

$$I = \int_a^\infty e^{-x} f(x) \, dx \qquad (31)$$

can be evaluated by a procedure known as Gauss-Laguerre integration. The difficulty with this method is that the points are not symmetrically distributed, so a solution with n points requires 2 n input parameters (n ξ_i's and n w_i's). The method sometimes requires a very large tabular input for a satisfactory level of accuracy; for example, a 20 point solution requires 40 numerical constants in the input. It is possible to break the interval into a finite part and an infinite part as in equation (30), then use the modified Gauss program for the finite part and Gauss-Laguerre integration for the infinite part.

An integral of the type

$$I = \int_{-\infty}^{\infty} e^{-x^2} f(x) \, dx \tag{32}$$

can be evaluated by Gauss-Hermite integration. In this procedure the points are symmetrically distributed, but there is another drawback. In most integrals of the type (32) which occur in practice, the lower limit is zero instead of $-\infty$. The two cases are not equivalent unless $f(x)$ happens to be an even function.

Problems

Evaluate the following integrals numerically. (Analytical results are given to make it easy to check the numerical evaluations.)

1. $\displaystyle\int_0^1 \frac{x^3}{1+x} \, dx = \frac{5}{6} - \ln 2$

2. $\displaystyle\int_0^1 \frac{dx}{1+x+x^2} = \frac{\pi}{3\sqrt{3}}$

3. $\displaystyle\int_0^1 \frac{dx}{x^2 + 5x + 6} = \ln \frac{9}{8}$

4. $\displaystyle\int_0^1 \frac{dx}{\sqrt{1+x^2}} = \ln(\sqrt{2}+1)$

5. $\displaystyle\int_0^{\pi/2} \left(\frac{x}{\sin x}\right)^2 dx = \pi \ln 2$

6. $\displaystyle\int_0^{\pi} \frac{dx}{(2+\cos x)^2} = \frac{2\pi}{3\sqrt{3}}$

7. $\displaystyle\int_0^{\pi} \frac{x \sin x}{1+\cos^2 x} \, dx = \frac{\pi^2}{4}$

8. $\displaystyle\int_0^{\pi/4} \ln(1+\tan x) \, dx = \frac{\pi}{8} \ln 2$

9. $\displaystyle\int_0^{\pi/2} \ln \sin x \, dx = -\frac{\pi}{2} \ln 2$

10. $\displaystyle\int_0^{\pi} x \ln \sin x \, dx = -\frac{\pi^2}{2}$

11. $\int_1^2 \dfrac{dx}{[(x-1)(2-x)]^{1/2}} = \pi$

12. $\int_1^2 \left(\dfrac{2-x}{x-1}\right)^{1/2} dx = \dfrac{\pi}{2}$

13. $\int_1^2 [(x-1)(2-x)]^{1/2}\, dx = \dfrac{\pi}{8}$

14. $\int_0^\infty \dfrac{dx}{x^4+1} = \dfrac{\pi}{2\sqrt{2}}$

15. $\int_0^\infty \dfrac{x\, dx}{e^x-1} = \dfrac{\pi^2}{6}$

16. $\int_0^\infty \dfrac{x\, dx}{e^{\alpha x}-1} \qquad \alpha = 0.5,\ 1.0,\ 1.5,\ 2.0,\ 2.5$

17. $\int_0^\infty \dfrac{x\, dx}{e^x+1} = \dfrac{\pi^2}{12}$

18. $\int_0^1 \dfrac{x \ln x}{1-x^2}\, dx = -\dfrac{\pi^2}{24}$

19. $\int_0^\infty \left(\dfrac{1}{e^x-1} - \dfrac{e^{-x}}{x}\right) dx = \gamma = .5772156649$

5

DIFFERENTIAL
EQUATIONS

1. First order differential equations

The Runge-Kutta method. This is one of the most widely used numerical methods of solving differential equations. We consider the general first order differential equation

$$\frac{dy}{dx} = y' = f(x,y) \tag{1}$$

Let the value of y be known at one point, say $y = y_i$ at $x = x_i$. Then the value of y at a neighboring point $i + 1$ is given by the equations*

$$q_1 = hf\,(x_i, y_i) \tag{2a}$$

$$q_2 = hf\left(x_i + \frac{h}{2}, y_i + \frac{q_1}{2}\right) \tag{2b}$$

$$q_3 = hf\left(x_i + \frac{h}{2}, y_i + \frac{q_2}{2}\right) \tag{2c}$$

$$q_4 = hf\,(x_i + h, y_i + q_3) \tag{2d}$$

$$y_{i+1} = y_i + \tfrac{1}{6}(q_1 + 2q_2 + 2q_3 + q_4) \tag{2e}$$

where h is the length of the interval. If the desired point is some distance from the starting point, the interval is divided into n increments of length h where

$$h = \frac{x_n - x_0}{n} \tag{3}$$

If f is a function of x only, it is clear that equations (2) reduce to Simpson's rule.

A program is given below for the Runge-Kutta solution of the equation

$$\frac{dy}{dx} = x + y \tag{4}$$

*All of the algorithms used in this chapter can be found in reference 3, pages 896–897, unless other references are specified. Derivations can be found in books on numerical analysis, e.g. reference 11. Also see section 2 of the appendix.

114

The program is straightforward. In line 1, h is calculated from equation (3). The parameters q_1, q_2, q_3, and q_4 are calculated in lines 2, 3, 4, and 5, respectively. The values of q or 2q are inserted into data register 08 as they are found. Line 6 calculates y_{i+1}. Line 7 creates a Dsz loop which carries the calculation forward from point 0 to points 1, 2, 3, ... , n. Line 8 is the function subroutine which represents equation (4). Since each q contains a factor of h, a multiplication by h has been included in the subroutine. Otherwise it would be necessary to perform the multiplication each of the four times that q appears in the main program. The program can be applied to any other first order equation by changing the subroutine in line 8.

0	LRN	000
1	RCL03 − RCL01 = ÷ RCL04 = STO05	012
2	RCL02 STO07 RCL01 STO06 SBR095 STO08	025
3	÷ 2 + RCL02 = STO07 RCL05 ÷ 2 = SUM06 SBR095 SUM08 SUM08	047
4	÷ 2 + RCL02 = STO07 SBR095 SUM08 SUM08	062
5	+ RCL02 = STO07 RCL05 SUM01 RCL01 STO06 SBR095 SUM08	081
6	RCL08 ÷ 6 = SUM02	088
7	2nd Dsz 4012 RCL02 R/S	095
8	RCL06 + RCL07 = × RCL05 = INV SBR	106
	LRN	

Contents of data registers

01 x_1 02 y_i 03 x_n 04 n − i   05 h   06 x   07 y
08 $q_1 + 2q_2 + 2q_3 + q_4$

Input/output

Press x_0 STO01 y_0 STO02 x_n STO03 n STO04 RST R/S

Display y_n

Results are given in the second column of the table below for the input data

$$x_0 = 0 \quad y_0 = 1 \quad x_n = .5, \quad 1.0, \quad 1.5, \quad 2.0$$
$$n = 5, \quad 10, \quad 15, \quad 20$$

Each value of n corresponds to the value of x_n directly above. The exact solution

$$y = 2e^x - x - 1$$

is shown in the first column for comparison.

x_n \ y_n	exact	Runge-Kutta	Adams	Milne
0.5	1.797443	1.797441	1.797442	1.797441
1.0	3.436564	3.436559	3.436561	3.436556
1.5	6.463378	6.463368	6.463371	6.463355
2.0	11.778112	11.778090	11.778095	11.778058

When the value of y is required at more than one point, it is not necessary to start the calculation at the original point x_0 each time. The program is set up so that at the end of a calculation the final values x_n and y_n are stored in the input data registers 01 and 02. This makes it easy to use the results of one calculation as the starting point for a subsequent calculation. Consider the example just given. We have found the value of y at x = .5. To find the value of y at the point x = 1.0, we leave the existing data in data registers 01 and 02 and punch the new value x_n = 1 into data register 03 and the desired value of n into data register 04. We again choose n = 5. The result is identical to the one given in the table. In the present example the calculation can be simplified a little further. Since the new increment is the same as the old increment (.1 in both cases), we can bypass line 1 of the program and obtain the result by pressing GT0012 R/S instead of RST R/S. Subsequent results are obtained in the same way. After the result at the point x = 1.0 has been found,

116

we obtain the result at the point x = 1.5 by pressing 1.5 STO03 5 STO04 GTO012 R/S.

The Runge-Kutta method has several advantages. It is easy to program and gives good accuracy. Also, the analysis for each increment is self-contained; results at the point i + 1 are found by using only data at the point i. Since the calculation does not require a knowledge of results at the left of the starting point, the procedure is self-starting. Also, it is possible to use different values of the increment length h in the same calculation; this is sometimes advantageous if the function f varies slowly in one region and rapidly in another region. However, the method has a major disadvantage. The function f(x,y) is evaluated four times in each cycle. For the simple differential equation (4) this is not objectionable. However, for a more complicated differential equation this requires a great deal of running time, and the method is inefficient.

The Adams method. It is sometimes more advantageous to use a different type of method in which the value of y at any point is expressed in terms of the values of f and y at several preceding points. One commonly used method of this type is the Adams method. The equations are

$$\phi_i = \frac{h}{24}(19f_i - 5f_{i-1} + f_{i-2}) \tag{5a}$$

$$y_{i+1} = y_i + \tfrac{3}{2}h\,(f_i - \tfrac{3}{2}f_{i-1} + f_{i-2} - \tfrac{1}{4}f_{i-3}) + \phi_i \tag{5b}$$

$$y_{i+1} = y_i + \tfrac{3}{8}h\,f_{i+1} + \phi_i \tag{5c}$$

Equations (5b) and 5(c) are the fundamental equations. Equation (5a) could be substituted into these, but the equations are algebraically simpler in the form shown. Equation (5b) is used first. This gives the value of y at the point i + 1 in terms of its value at i and the values of f at points i, i − 1, i − 2, and i − 3. The method cannot be used to start an analysis; it is always necessary to have the values of f at three points to the left of the increment being considered. This can be done by using the Runge-Kutta method for the first three increments. The analysis is then switched to the Adams method. Equation (5b) is not sufficiently accurate to give satisfactory results for most problems. Equation (5c) is more accurate, but it cannot be used directly because the term f_{i+1} on the right side is not known until after y_{i+1} has been evaluated. The procedure is to use equation (5b) first to obtain a preliminary estimate of y_{i+1}. The corresponding value of f_{i+1} is found from the function $f(x,y)$ defined by the differential equation. This will appear as a subroutine at the end of the program. An improved value of y_{i+1} is then found from equation (5c). This type of method is known as a predictor-corrector method. Equation (5b) is the predictor and equation (5c) is the corrector. This method is much more efficient than the Runge-Kutta method, because the function subroutine is used only once in each cycle instead of four times.

The program appears below. The first half is essentially the same as the Runge-Kutta program, but there are a few additions. Line 1 calculates h and also stores the number 3 in data register 00. This is used as a counter for the Runge-Kutta segment of the program, which consists of a Dsz loop which runs from line 2 to line 9. Line 2 calculates q_1, which is also hf_i. Line 3 stores this in preparation for the Adams segment of the program. The exchange procedure of chapter 1, section 5, is used. At the end of three Runge-Kutta cycles, the parameters hf_0, hf_1, hf_2 are stored in data registers 09, 10, and 11, respectively. These then become hf_{i-3}, hf_{i-2}, hf_{i-1}. Lines, 4, 5, and 6 calculate q_2, q_3, and q_4, respectively. The values of q or 2q are inserted into data register 08 as they are found. Line 7 calculates y_{i+1}. Line 8 deducts 1 from the counter for the Adams segment, which is stored in data register 04. This is necessary so that the total number of cycles in the program will be correct. Line 9 executes the Dsz loop and completes the Runge-Kutta segment of the program. In line 10, hf_3 is calculated and stored in data register 12. This then becomes hf_i. The Adams segment of the program is a Dsz loop which runs from line 11 to line 16. Lines 11 and 12 represent equations (5a) and (5b), respectively. Line 13 calculates hf_{i+1}. Line 14 shifts the hf's to new data registers in preparation for the next cycle. The parameters f_{i+1}, f_i, f_{i-1}, and f_{i-2} become f_i, f_{i-1}, f_{i-2}, and f_{i-3}, respectively. Line 15 represents equation (5c). Line 16 creates a Dsz loop. Line 17 is the function subroutine for equation (4). Since the function f is always multiplied by h wherever it appears in equations (5) as well as (2), we have included the multiplication in the subroutine instead of performing it repeatedly in the main program.

```
0   LRN                                              000

1   RCL03 − RCL01 = ÷ RCL04 = STO05   3STO00    015

2   RCL02   STO07   RCL01   STO06   SBR201
    STO08                                            028
```

3	2nd Exc 11 2nd Exc 10 STO09	034
4	RCL11 $\div$ 2 + RCL02 = STO07 RCL05 $\div$ 2 = SUM06 SBR201 SUM08 SUM08	058
5	$\div$ 2 + RCL02 = STO07 SBR201 SUM08 SUM08	073
6	+ RCL02 = STO07 RCL05 SUM01 RCL01 STO06 SBR201 SUM08	092
7	RCL08 $\div$ 6 = SUM02	099
8	2nd Op 34	101
9	2nd Dsz 0015	105
10	RCL02 STO07 SBR201 STO12	114
11	19 $\times$ RCL12 $-$ 5 $\times$ RCL11 + RCL10 = $\div$ 24 = STO13	134
12	RCL12 $-$ 1.5 $\times$ RCL11 + RCL10 $-$ RCL09 $\div$ 4 = $\times$ 1.5 + RCL13 + RCL02 = STO07	165
13	RCL05 SUM01 SUM06 SBR201	174
14	2nd Exc 12 2nd Exc 11 2nd Exc 10 STO09	182
15	RCL12 $\times$ 3 $\div$ 8 + RCL13 = SUM02	194
16	2nd Dsz 4114 RCL02 R/S	201
17	RCL06 + RCL07 = $\times$ RCL05 = INV SBR	212
	LRN	

Contents of data registers

00 $3 - i$ 01 x_i 02 y_i 03 x_n 04 $n - i$ 05 h   06 x
07 y   08 $q_1 + 2q_2 + 2q_3 + q_4$ 09 hf_{i-3} 10 hf_{i-2}
11 hf_{i-1} 12 hf_i 13 ϕ_i

Input/output

Press x_0 STO01 y_0 STO02 x_n STO03   n STO04   RST
         R/S

Display x_n

Numerical results appear in the third column of the table given
earlier. The same remarks about obtaining results after the first result
which were made for the Runge-Kutta method apply here also. To
obtain the value of y at x = 1, we use the results at x = .5 as input
and punch in the additional data 1 STO03 5 STO04. Then, since
the increment is again .1, we can bypass the Runge-Kutta starting
segment of the program and press GTO114 R/S.

There is one important difference in input between the Runge-
Kutta method and a method of the predictor-corrector type. In using
the Runge-Kutta method, we have a free choice of h for each part
of the analysis. We happened to choose a constant value h = .1 throughout. In the present method there is no convenient way to change h
during the analysis, since the calculations at each point use data from
preceding points.

The Milne method. Another widely used predictor-corrector method
is the Milne method. The predictor equation is

$$y_{i+1} = y_{i-3} + \tfrac{4}{3} h (2f_i - f_{i-1} + 2f_{i-2}) \qquad (6a)$$

and the corrector equation is

$$y_{i+1} = y_{i-1} + \frac{h}{3} (f_{i+1} + 4f_i + f_{i-1}) \qquad (6b)$$

The Milne equations are simpler than the Adams equations. However,
this advantage is partially offset by the y_{i-3} term in the predictor
equation. This term makes it necessary to store several y's as well
as f's.

The program appears below. The first half is essentially the same
as the Runge-Kutta program, but there are several additions. Line 1
calculates h and also stores the number 3 in data register 00. This
is used as a counter for the Runge-Kutta segment of the program,
which consists of a Dsz loop that runs from line 2 to line 9. Line 2
recalls y_i and stores it in preparation for the Milne segment of the
program. The exchange procedure of chapter 1, section 5, is used.

Line 3 calculates q_1, which is also hf_i, and stores it in preparation for the Milne segment of the program. Lines 4, 5, and 6 calculate q_2, q_3, and q_4, respectively. The values of q or 2q are inserted into data register 08 as they are found. Line 7 calculates y_{i+1}. Line 8 deducts 1 from the counter for the Milne segment, which is stored in data register 04. This is necessary so that the total number of cycles in the program will be correct. Line 9 completes the Runge-Kutta segment of the program. Line 10 calculates hf_3, which then becomes hf_i. The Milne segment of the program is a Dsz loop that runs from line 11 to line 16. Line 11 represents equation (6a), line 12 calculates hf_{i+1}, and line 13 represents equation (6b). In lines 14 and 15 the y's and hf's are shifted to different data registers in preparation for the next cycle. Line 16 creates a Dsz loop. Line 17 is the function subroutine for equation (4).

0	LRN	000
1	RCL03 − RCL01 = ÷ RCL04 = STO05 3 STO00	015
2	RCL02 STO07 2nd Exc 11 2nd Exc 10 STO09	025
3	RCL01 STO06 SBR188 STO08 2nd Exc 13 STO12	038
4	RCL13 ÷ 2 + RCL02 = STO07 RCL05 ÷ 2 = SUM06 SBR188 SUM08 SUM08	062
5	÷ 2 + RCL02 = STO07 SBR188 SUM08 SUM08	077
6	+ RCL02 = STO07 RCL05 SUM01 RCL01 STO06 SBR188 SUM08	096
7	RCL08 ÷ 6 = SUM02	103
8	2nd Op 34	105
9	2nd Dsz 0015	109
10	RCL02 STO07 SBR188 STO14	118

11	RCL14 − RCL13 ÷ 2 + RCL12 = × 8 ÷ 3 + RCL09 = STO07	139
12	RCL05 SUM01 SUM06 SBR188 STO15	150
13	+ 4 × RCL14 + RCL13 = ÷ 3 + RCL11 =	165
14	2nd Exc 02 2nd Exc 11 2nd Exc 10 STO09	173
15	RCL15 2nd Exc 14 2nd Exc 13 STO12	181
16	2nd Dsz 4118 RCL02 R/S	188
17	RCL06 + RCL07 = × RCL05 = INV SBR	199
	LRN	

Contents of data registers

00 $3-i$ 01 x_i 02 y_i 03 x_n 04 $n-i$ 05 h 06 x 07 y
08 $q_1 + 2q_2 + 2q_3 + q_4$ 09 y_{i-3} 10 y_{i-2} 11 y_{i-1} 12 hf_{i-2}
13 hf_{i-1} 14 hf_i 15 hf_{i+1}

Input/output

Press x_0 STO01 y_0 STO02 x_n STO03 n STO04 RST
       R/S

Display y_n

Numerical results appear in the fourth column of the table given earlier in this section. The same remarks about obtaining results after the first that were made for the two previous programs apply here also. For example, after the value of y has been found at the point x = .5, we obtain the value of y at the point x = 1.0 by pressing 1 STO03 5 STO04 GTO118 R/S.

It was pointed out earlier that the most straightforward way of writing a program is not always the most efficient. The foregoing program provides another example of this. In writing the program, we have assigned an individual data register to each parameter. This makes the program straightforward and easy to follow, but it does not make the most efficient use of the available data storage space.

Inspection of the program shows that the data registers 00 and 08 are used only in the Runge-Kutta segment, which ends with line 9. On the other hand, the data registers 14 and 15, which contain the parameters hf_i and hf_{i+1}, are used only in the latter part of the program, starting with line 10. Also, the data register 03 is addressed only in line 1, whereas the data register 13, which contains the parameter hf_{i-1}, appears for the first time in line 3. Instead of opening data registers 13, 14, and 15, we could reuse data registers 03, 00, and 08 to accommodate hf_{i-1}, hf_i, and hf_{i+1}, respectively. This is accomplished by simply replacing the addresses 13, 14, and 15 by 03, 00, and 08 wherever they appear in the program. The modified program operates in exactly the same way as the original one, but it uses only thirteen data registers instead of sixteen. This trick will not be needed for any of the programs in this book, but it is sometimes useful when the number of parameters exceeds the number of available data registers.

Accuracy of numerical solutions. Iteration is sometimes used to improve the accuracy of predictor-corrector methods. Consider the Adams method. After y_{i+1} has been calculated from equation (5c) in line 15 of the program, it is possible to run the subroutine again with the new value of y_{i+1} and obtain an improved value of f_{i+1}. The calculation with equation (5c) is then repeated, using the improved value of f_{i+1} to obtain a more accurate value of y_{i+1}. This cycle can be repeated as many times as desired. However, this refinement increases the length and running time of the program, and it does not guarantee accurate results. The iterations do not approach the exact result because equation (5c) is not exact; it has an inherent error for any value of h greater than zero. If highly accurate results are desired, the most effective and reliable procedure is to reduce the value of h. In all of the methods of this chapter, the error per step is of order h^5, and the error for the entire interval is of order h^4, that is of order n^{-4}. As a result the accuracy of the results improves rapidly as n is increased. However, this procedure cannot be continued indefinitely because the accuracy of the results is eventually limited by roundoff error.

Normally results approach the exact values as $h \to 0$ (with the exception of roundoff errors). However, it occasionally happens that a numerical evaluation breaks down, and no satisfactory result can be obtained. Extensive discussions of this problem can be found in books on numerical analysis. Here we simply state that the frequency with which difficulties occur depends upon the method used. Generally the Runge-Kutta and Adams methods are highly reliable; anomalous results seldom occur in problems of practical interest. The Milne method is somewhat less reliable.

Occasionally a numerical solution may be unstable because of a peculiarity in the differential equation and the initial conditions regardless of the computational method used. A simple heuristic discussion may clarify this problem. Consider the differential equation (4). The analytical solution is

$$y = Ae^x - x - 1$$

where A is a numerical constant. Suppose that the initial condition is $y = -1$ at $x = 0$. Then $A = 0$. However, if we carry out a numerical evaluation and fit the analytical solution to the resulting points, we will obtain a value of A which is very small but not identically zero. If the numerical evaluation is continued to very large values of x, the spurious exponential term will eventually overshadow the legitimate terms, and the solution will break down.

2. General second order differential equations

The Runge-Kutta method. The most common method of solving a higher order differential equation is to write the equation as a set of simultaneous first order equations. However, there is a direct Runge-Kutta algorithm for a second order differential equation which leads to a shorter program than the use of simultaneous equations. Consider the general second order equation

$$\frac{d^2y}{dx^2} = y'' = f(x,y) \tag{7}$$

The appropriate Runge-Kutta equations are

$$q_1 = hf(x_i, y_i, y_i') \tag{8a}$$

$$q_2 = hf\left(x_i + \frac{h}{2}, y_i + \frac{h}{2}y_i' + \frac{h}{8}q_1, y_i' + \frac{q_1}{2}\right) \tag{8b}$$

$$q_3 = hf\left(x_i + \frac{h}{2}, y_i + \frac{h}{2}y_i' + \frac{h}{8}q_1, y_i' + \frac{q_2}{2}\right) \tag{8c}$$

$$q_4 = hf\left(x_i + h, y_i + hy_i' + \frac{h}{2}q_3, y_i' + q_3\right) \tag{8d}$$

$$y_{i+1} = y_i + h\,[y_i' + \tfrac{1}{6}\,(q_1 + q_2 + q_3)] \qquad (8e)$$

$$y_{i+1}' = y_i' + \tfrac{1}{6}\,(q_1 + 2q_2 + 2q_3 + q_4) \qquad (8f)$$

A program follows for the Runge-Kutta solution of the equation

$$\frac{d^2y}{dx^2} - 3\frac{dy}{dx} + 2y = x \qquad \text{or} \qquad y'' = 3y' - 2y + x \qquad (9)$$

The program is straightforward. In line 1, h is calculated from equation (3). The parameter q_1 is calculated in line 2, q_2 is calculated in lines 3 and 4, q_3 is calculated in line 5, and q_4 is calculated in lines 6 and 7. The values of q are inserted into data registers 10 and 11 as they are found. y_{i+1} is calculated in line 8, and y_{i+1}' is calculated in line 9. Line 10 creates a Dsz loop, and line 11 is the function subroutine which represents equation (9). The same program can be applied to any other second order differential equation by revising line 11.

0	LRN	000
1	RCL04 − RCL01 = ÷ RCL05 = STO06	012
2	RCL03 STO09 RCL02 STO08 RCL01 STO07 SBR145 STO10	029
3	÷ 2 + RCL03 = STO09 + RCL03 = × RCL06 ÷ 4 + RCL02 = STO08	052
4	RCL06 ÷ 2 = SUM07 SBR145 SUM10 STO11	066
5	÷ 2 + RCL03 = STO09 SBR145 SUM10 SUM11	081
6	+ RCL03 = STO09 + RCL03 = × RCL06 ÷ 2 + RCL02 = STO08	102
7	RCL06 SUM01 RCL01 STO07 SBR145 SUM11	115
8	RCL10 SUM11 ÷ 6 + RCL03 = × RCL06 = SUM02	131

125

9   RCL11 ÷ 6 = SUM03   138

10 2nd Dsz 5012   RCL02   R/S   145

11 RCL07 − 2 × RCL08 + 3 × RCL09 = × RCL06 =
    INV SBR   163

    LRN

Contents of data registers

01 x_i 02 y_i 03 y_i' 04 x_n 05 $n-i$ 06 h 07 x 08 y
09 y' 10 $q_1 + q_2 + q_3$ 11 $q_1 + 2q_2 + 2q_3 + q_4$

Input/output

Press x_0 STO01 y_0 STO02 y_0' STO03 x_n STO04   n STO05
RST   R/S

Display y_n

If y_n' is required, this is obtained by pressing RCL03.

Results appear in the second column of the table below for the input data

$x_0 = 0$ $y_0 = 1$ $y_0' = 1$ $x_n = .5,$ 1.0,   1.5,   2.0
                                         $n = 5,$ 10,   15,   20

Each value of n corresponds to the value of x_n directly above. The exact solution

$$y = \tfrac{1}{4}(e^{2x} + 2x + 3)$$

is shown in the first column for comparison.

x_n \ y_n	exact	Runge-Kutta	Milne	Adams
0.5	1.679570	1.679551	1.679556	1.679556
1.0	3.097264	3.097131	3.097101	3.097115
1.5	6.521384	6.520763	6.520364	6.520455
2.0	15.399538	15.397173	15.394768	15.395218

The same remarks about obtaining results after the first which were made in section 1 apply here also. For example, after the value of y has been found at the point x = .5, we obtain the value of y at the point x = 1.0 by pressing 1 STO04   5 STO05   GTO012   R/S.

The foregoing program can be used to solve a pair of simultaneous first order differential equations. The equations must first be combined algebraically into one second order equation. A Runge-Kutta program which solves two simultaneous first order equations directly is given in reference 13, pages 3–14 to 3–25. However, this program is twice as long as the one given here.

The Milne method. Predictor–corrector methods can also be applied to higher order differential equations. Milne's method is the easiest to use because it has the simplest equations. With either the Milne or Adams method it is necessary to store several values of f and y′. The same Milne relations (6) which connect y with y′ for a first order equation now connect y with y′ and y′ with y′′. For the second order equation (7), we have

$$y'_{i+1} = y'_{i-3} + \frac{4h}{3}(2f_i - f_{i-1} + 2f_{i-2}) \tag{10a}$$

$$y_{i+1} = y_{i-1} + \frac{h}{3}(y'_{i+1} + 4y'_i + y'_{i-1}) \tag{10b}$$

$$y'_{i+1} = y'_{i-1} + \frac{h}{3}(f_{i+1} + 4f_i + f_{i-1}) \tag{10c}$$

Equation (10a) is a predictor equation; equations (10b) and (10c) are corrector-type equations. It is not necessary to use a predictor equation for y_{i+1}. After a preliminary estimate of y'_{i+1} is obtained from equation (10a), an accurate value of y_{i+1} is obtained directly from equation (10b). f_{i+1} is then found from the function subroutine, and an accurate value of y'_{i+1} is found from equation (10c).

The program appears below. A preliminary operation is necessary. Normally the TI-58 calculator has a capacity of 30 data registers and 240 program steps. Because of the length of the present program, it is necessary to repartition the memory as discussed in chapter 1, section 7. This is accomplished by pressing 2 2nd Op 17. This results in a capacity of 20 data registers and 320 program steps. If the TI-59 calculator is used, this repartitioning is not necessary.

The first part of the program proper is essentially the same as the Runge-Kutta program, but there are several additions. Line 1 calculates h and also stores the number 3 in data register 00. This is used as a counter for the Runge-Kutta segment of the program, which consists of a Dsz loop which runs from line 2 to line 13. Lines 2, 3, and 4 calculate q_1, which is also hf_i. At the same time the values of y_i', y_i, and hf_i which will be needed in the Milne calculations are stored in lines 2, 3, and 4, respectively. Lines 5 and 6 calculate q_2, line 7 calculates q_3, and lines 8 and 9 calculate q_4. The values of the q's are inserted into data registers 10 and 11 as they are found. Lines 10 and 11 calculate y_i and y_i', respectively. Line 12 deducts 1 from the counter for the Milne segment, which is stored in data register 05, so that the total number of cycles for the program will be correct. Line 13 completes the Runge-Kutta segment of the program. Line 14 calculates hf_3, which then become hf_i. The Milne segment of the program is a Dsz loop which runs from line 15 to line 22. Lines 15 and 16 represent equations (10a) and (10b), respectively. Line 17 calculates hf_{i+1}, and line 18 represents equation (10c). The values of y', y, and hf are shifted to new data registers in lines 19, 20, and 21, respectively, in preparation for the next cycle. Line 22 executes the Dsz loop and completes the Milne segment of the program. Line 23 is the function subroutine for equation (9).

2 2nd Op 17

0	LRN				000
1	RCL04 − RCL01 = ÷ RCL05 = ST006 3 ST000				015
2	RCL03 ST009 2nd Exc 15 2nd Exc 14 ST013				025
3	RCL02 ST008 ST012				031
4	RCL01 ST007 SBR270 ST010 2nd Exc 17 ST016				044
5	RCL17 ÷ 2 + RCL03 = ST009 + RCL03 = × RCL06 ÷ 4 + RCL02 = ST008				069
6	RCL06 ÷ 2 = SUM07 SBR270 SUM10 ST011				083

7   ÷ 2 + RCL03 = STO09   SBR270   SUM10
       SUM11   098

8   + RCL03 = STO09 + RCL03 = × RCL06 ÷ 2 +
       RCL02 = STO08   119

9   RCL06   SUM01   RCL01   STO07   SBR270
       SUM11   132

10   RCL10   SUM11 ÷ 6 + RCL03 = × RCL06 =
       SUM02   148

11   RCL11 ÷ 6 = SUM03   155

12   2nd Op 35   157

13   2nd Dsz 0015   161

14   RCL03   STO09   RCL02   STO08   SBR270
       STO18   174

15   RCL18 − RCL17 ÷ 2 + RCL16 = × 8 ÷ 3 +
       RCL13 = STO09   195

16   + 4 × RCL03 + RCL15 = ÷ 3 × RCL06 +
       RCL12 = STO08   215

17   RCL06   SUM01   SUM07   SBR270   STO19   226

18   + 4 × RCL18 + RCL17 = ÷ 3 + RCL15 =   241

19   2nd Exc 03   2nd Exc 15   2nd Exc 14   STO13   249

20   RCL08   2nd Exc 02   STO12   255

21   RCL19   2nd Exc 18   2nd Exc 17   STO16   263

22   2nd Dsz 5174   RCL02   R/S   270

23   RCL07 − 2 × RCL08 + 3 × RCL09 = × RCL06 =
       INV SBR   288

       LRN

Contents of data registers

00 $3 - i$ 01 x_i 02 y_i 03 y_i' 04 x_n 05 $n - i$ 06 h 07 x
08 y 09 y' 10 $q_1 + q_2 + q_3$ 11 $q_1 + 2q_2 + 2q_3 + q_4$ 12 y_{i-1}
13 y_{i-3}' 14 y_{i-2}' 15 y_{i-1}' 16 hf_{i-2} 17 hf_{i-1} 18 hf_i 19 hf_{i+1}

Input/output

Press x_0 STO01 y_0 STO02 y_0' STO03 x_n STO04
n STO05   RST   R/S

Display y_n

If y_n' is required, this is obtained by pressing RCL03.

Numerical results appear in the third column of the table given earlier in this section. The same remarks about obtaining results after the first that were made for the earlier program apply here also. For example, after the value of y has been found at the point x = .5, we obtain the value of y at the point x = 1.0 by pressing 1 STO04 5 STO05   GTO174   R/S.

The Adams method. The Adams method can also be applied to higher order differential equations. Equations (5), adapted to a second order differential equation, become

$$\phi_i = \frac{h}{24} (19f_i - 5f_{i-1} + f_{i-2}) \tag{11a}$$

$$y_{i+1}' = y_i' + \frac{3}{2} h \left(f_i - \frac{3}{2} f_{i-1} + f_{i-2} - \frac{1}{4} f_{i-3} \right) + \phi_i \tag{11b}$$

$$y_{i+1} = y_i + \frac{h}{24} (9y_{i+1}' + 19y_i' - 5y_{i-1}' + y_{i-2}') \tag{11c}$$

$$y_{i+1}' = y_i' + \frac{3}{8} hf_{i+1} + \phi_i \tag{11d}$$

The program appears below. It is constructed in the same way as the earlier predictor–corrector programs. It is considerably longer than the Milne program. In fact, for the differential equation (9), the length of the Adams program is just barely within the capacity of the TI-

58 calculator. Programs for more complicated differential equations will run only on the TI-59. When this calculator is used, the preliminary repartitioning is not necessary.

2 2nd Op 17

0	LRN	000
1	RCL04 − RCL01 = ÷ RCL05 = STO06 3 STO00	015
2	RCL03 STO09 2nd Exc 13 STO12	023
3	RCL02 STO08 RCL01 STO07 SBR299 STO10	036
4	2nd Exc 16 2nd Exc 15 STO14	042
5	RCL16 ÷ 2 + RCL03 = STO09 + RCL03 = × RCL06 ÷ 4 + RCL02 = STO08	067
6	RCL06 ÷ 2 = SUM07 SBR299 SUM10 STO11	081
7	÷ 2 + RCL03 = STO09 SBR299 SUM10 SUM11	096
8	+ RCL03 = STO09 + RCL03 = × RCL06 ÷ 2 + RCL02 = STO08	117
9	RCL06 SUM01 RCL01 STO07 SBR299 SUM11	130
10	RCL10 SUM11 ÷ 6 + RCL03 = × RCL06 = SUM02	146
11	RCL11 ÷ 6 = SUM03	153
12	2nd Op 35	155
13	2nd Dsz 0015	159
14	RCL03 STO09 RCL02 STO08 SBR299 STO17	172

15 $19 \times RCL17 - 5 \times RCL16 + RCL15 = \div 24 =$
    STO18   192

16 $RCL17 - 1.5 \times RCL16 + RCL15 - RCL14 \div 4 =$
    $\times 1.5 + RCL18 + RCL03 = STO09$ 223

17 $\times 9 + 19 \times RCL03 - 5 \times RCL13 + RCL12 =$
    $\times RCL06 \div 24 + RCL02 = STO08$ 252

18 RCL06   SUM01   SUM07   SBR299   261

19 2nd Exc 17   2nd Exc 16   2nd Exc 15   STO14   269

20 $RCL17 \times 3 \div 8 + RCL03 + RCL18 =$ 282

21 2nd Exc 03   2nd Exc 13   STO12   288

22 RCL08   STO02   292

23 2nd Dsz 5172   RCL02   R/S   299

24 $RCL07 - 2 \times RCL08 + 3 \times RCL09 = \times RCL06 =$
    INV SBR   317

    LRN

Contents of data registers

00 $3 - i$ 01 x_i 02 y_i 03 y_i' 04 x_n 05 $n - i$ 06 h 07 x
08 y 09 y' 10 $q_1 + q_2 + q_3$ 11 $q_1 + 2q_2 + 2q_3 + q_4$
12 y_{i-2}' 13 y_{i-1}' 14 hf_{i-3} 15 hf_{i-2} 16 hf_{i-1} 17 hf_i 18 ϕ_i

The input/output procedure for the initial calculation is identical
to the one given earlier for the first two programs of this section.
Numerical results appear in the table given near the beginning of
the section. The same remarks about obtaining results after the first
which were made for the earlier programs obtain here also. For example, after the value of y has been found at the point x = .5, we obtain
the value of y at the point x = 1.0 by pressing 1 STO04
5 STO05   GTO172   R/S.

3. Special second order differential equations

  Many physical problems are represented by differential equations which contain only derivatives of even order. Thus equation (7) can often be simplified to

$$y'' = f(x,y) \tag{12}$$

Equations of this type are sometimes known as special differential equations. They can of course be solved by using the general programs of section 2. However, since it is possible to write programs for this case which are shorter and simpler than the general programs, we shall consider this case separately. The programs are constructed in the same way as those considered earlier, so we shall give them without comment.

The Runge-Kutta method. For equation (12), the Runge-Kutta equations (8) can be simplified to

$$q_1 = hf(x_i, y_i) \tag{13a}$$

$$q_2 = hf\left(x_i + \frac{h}{2}, \, y_i + \frac{h}{2}y_i' + \frac{h}{8}q_1\right) \tag{13b}$$

$$q_3 = hf\left(x_i + h, \, y_i + hy_i' + \frac{h}{2}q_2\right) \tag{13c}$$

$$y_{i+1} = y_i + h\left[y_i' + \tfrac{1}{6}(q_1 + 2q_2)\right] \tag{13d}$$

$$y_{i+1}' = y_i' + \tfrac{1}{6}(q_1 + 4q_2 + q_3) \tag{13e}$$

  A Runge-Kutta program for the equation

$$\frac{d^2y}{dx^2} = x + y \tag{14}$$

is given below.

0   LRN   000

1   RCL04 − RCL01 = ÷ RCL05 = STO06   012

2   RCL02   STO08   RCL01   STO07   SBR117
    STO09   025

3   ÷ 4 + RCL03 = × RCL06 ÷ 2 + RCL02 = STO08   042

4   RCL06 ÷ 2 = SUM07   SBR117 × 2 = SUM09
    STO10   059

5   ÷ 4 + RCL03 = × RCL06 + RCL02 = STO08   074

6   RCL06   SUM01   RCL01   STO07   SBR117
    SUM10   087

7   RCL09   SUM10 ÷ 6 + RCL03 = × RCL06 =
    SUM02   103

8   RCL10 ÷ 6 = SUM03   110

9   2nd Dsz 5012   RCL02   R/S   117

10 RCL07 + RCL08 = × RCL06 = INV SBR   128

    LRN

Contents of data registers

01 x_i 02 y_i 03 y_i' 04 x_n 05 $n-i$ 06 h   07 x   08 y
09 $q_1 + 2q_2$ 10 $q_1 + 4q_2 + q_3$

Input/output

Press x_0 STO01 y_0 STO02 y_0' STO03 x_n STO04
n STO05   RST   R/S

Display y_n

If y_n' is required, it is obtained by pressing RCL03.

134

Numerical results appear in the second column of the table below for $x_0 = 0$, $y_0 = 1$, $y_0' = 0$, and various values of x_n. The increment is $h = .1$ in all cases. The exact solution

$$y = e^x - x$$

is shown for comparison in the first column.

x_n $\diagdown$ y_n	exact	Runge-Kutta	Milne
0.5	1.148721	1.148721	1.148721
1.0	1.718282	1.718280	1.718281
1.5	2.981689	2.981686	2.981688
2.0	5.389056	5.389050	5.389054

The Milne method. In section 2 we applied the Milne method to the general second order differential equation (7) and obtained simultaneous equations which connect y with y' and y' with f. For the special second order equation (12), there is another Milne algorithm which bypasses the calculation of y' and gives a direct relation between y and f. The predictor equation is

$$y_{i+1} = 2y_{i-1} - y_{i-3} + \tfrac{4}{3}h^2 \, (f_i + f_{i-1} + f_{i-2})\tag{15a}$$

and the corrector equation is

$$y_{i+1} = 2y_i - y_{i-1} + \frac{h^2}{12} \, (f_{i+1} + 10f_i + f_{i-1})\tag{15b}$$

The program for equation (14) appears below.

```
        2 2nd Op 17

  0  LRN                                                  000

  1  RCL04 − RCL01 = ÷ RCL05 = STO06   3 STO00            015

  2  RCL02   STO08   2nd Exc 13   2nd Exc 12
     STO11                                                025

  3  RCL01   STO07   SBR226   STO09                       034
```

4 2nd Exc 15   STO14   038

5 RCL15 ÷ 4 + RCL03 = × RCL06 ÷ 2 + RCL02 =
   STO08   057

6 RCL06 ÷ 2 = SUM07   SBR226 × 2 = SUM09
   STO10   074

7 ÷ 4 + RCL03 = × RCL06 + RCL02 = STO08   089

8 RCL06   SUM01   RCL01   STO07   SBR226
   SUM10   102

9 RCL09   SUM10 ÷ 6 + RCL03 = ×RCL06 =
   SUM02   118

10 RCL10 ÷ 6 = SUM03   125

11 2nd Op 35   127

12 2nd Dsz 0015   131

13 RCL02   STO08   SBR226   STO16   140

14 RCL16 + RCL15 + RCL14 = × RCL06 × 4 ÷ 3 −
    RCL11 + 2 × RCL13 = STO08   167

15 RCL06   SUM01   SUM07   SBR226   STO17   178

16 + 10 × RCL16 + RCL15 = × RCL06 ÷ 12 −
    RCL13 + 2 × RCL02 =   203

17 2nd Exc 02   2nd Exc 13   2nd Exc 12   STO11   211

18 RCL17   2nd Exc 16   2nd Exc 15   STO14   219

19 2nd Dsz 5140   RCL02   R/S   226

20 RCL07 + RCL08 = × RCL06 = INV SBR   237

    LRN

Contents of data registers

136

00 $3-i$ 01 x_i 02 y_i 03 y_i' 04 x_n 05 $n-i$ 06 h 07 x

08 y 09 $q_1 + 2q_2$ 10 $q_1 + 4q_2 + q_3$ 11 y_{i-3} 12 y_{i-2}

13 y_{i-1} 14 hf_{i-2} 15 hf_{i-1} 16 hf_i 17 hf_{i+1}

Input/output

Press x_0 STO01 y_0 STO02 y_0' STO03 x_n STO04
        n STO05   RST   R/S

Display y_n

Numerical results appear in the third column of the table given earlier in this section.

The special Milne program has a limitation that sometimes restricts its usefulness. The value of y_i' is not calculated anywhere in the program. This shortens the calculation, but it also means that the output does not include the value of y_n'. In most applications this is not required. If it is, either the special Runge-Kutta program or one of the general programs of section 2 may be used.

4. Fourth order differential equations

There are several possible methods of obtaining a Runge-Kutta algorithm for a fourth order differential equation. One commonly used procedure is to write it as a set of four simultaneous first order equations. A direct algorithm analogous to that used in section 2 for the second order equation is also available. However, the simplest program is obtained by breaking the fourth order equation into two simultaneous second order equations, then using the results of section 2. We consider the general fourth order equation

$$\frac{d^4y}{dx^4} = y^{IV} = f(x,y,y',\ y'',\ y''') \tag{16}$$

and rewrite it as a pair of second order equations. Thus

$$z'' = f(x,y,y',z,z') \qquad y'' = z \tag{17}$$

From equations (8) and (17) we derive a set of equations that can be written in the form

$$q_1 = hf(x_i, y_i, y_i', y_i'', y_i''') \tag{18a}$$

$$r_1 = y_i'' + \frac{h}{2} y_i''' + \frac{h}{8} q_1 \tag{18b}$$

$$q_2 = hf\left(x_i + \frac{h}{2}, \ y_i + \frac{h}{2} y_i' + \frac{h^2}{8} y_i'', \ y_i' + \frac{h}{2} y_i'', \ r_1, \ y_i''' + \frac{q_1}{2}\right) \tag{18c}$$

$$q_3 = hf\left(\quad '' \quad , \quad\quad '' \quad\quad , \ y_i' + \frac{h}{2} r_1, \quad '', \ y_i''' + \frac{q_2}{2}\right) \tag{18d}$$

$$r_2 = y_i'' + h y_i''' + \frac{h}{2} q_3 \tag{18e}$$

$$s = y_i + h y_i' + \frac{h^2}{2} r_1 \tag{18f}$$

$$q_4 = hf(x_i + h, \ s, \ y_i' + h r_1, \ r_2, \ y_i''' + q_3) \tag{18g}$$

$$y_{i+1} = s + \frac{h^2}{6} (y_i'' - r_1) \tag{18h}$$

$$y_{i+1}' = y_i' + \frac{h}{6} (y_i'' + 4 r_1 + r_2) \tag{18i}$$

$$y_i'' = y_i'' + h[y_i''' + \tfrac{1}{6} (q_1 + q_2 + q_3)] \tag{18j}$$

$$y_i''' = y_i''' + \tfrac{1}{6} (q_1 + 2 q_2 + 2 q_3 + q_4) \tag{18k}$$

The program follows. Like the Milne program of section 2, it contains more than 240 steps, so we start by repartitioning the memory. (This step is necessary only with the TI-58; it may be omitted if the TI-59 is used.) In line 1, h is calculated from equation (3). q_1 is calculated in lines 2 and 3, and q_2 is calculated in lines 4 through 6. The parameter r_1 is obtained as an intermediate step in the evaluation of q_2. q_3 is calculated in lines 7 and 8, and q_4 is calculated in lines 9 through 11. The parameters r_2 and s are obtained as intermediate steps in the evaluation of q_4. The values of q are inserted into data registers 14 and 15 as they are found. y_{i+1}, y_{i+1}', y_{i+1}'', and y_{i+1}''' are calculated in lines 12, 13, 14, and 15, respectively. Line 16 creates a Dsz loop. Line 17 is the function subroutine for the equation

138

$$\frac{d^4y}{dx^4} - 2\frac{d^3y}{dx^3} + 3\frac{d^2y}{dx^2} - 5\frac{dy}{dx} + 3y = 0 \qquad (19)$$

A comment about the parameters r_1, r_2, and s may be desirable. r_1 is the value of y″ that is used in the evaluation of q_2. This is needed later, so it is stored in data register 16, since the value in data register 12 will be overwritten when subsequent values of y′ are calculated. On the other hand, the parameters r_2 and s appear near the end of the cycle. These may be left in the data registers 10 and 12 where they appear, since nothing else will be stored in these registers later.

2 2nd Op 17

0	LRN	000
1	RCL06 − RCL01 = ÷ RCL07 = STO08	012
2	RCL05 STO13 RCL04 STO12 RCL03 STO11	024
3	RCL02 STO10 RCL01 STO09 SBR259 STO14	037
4	÷ 2 + RCL05 = STO13 + RCL05 = × RCL08 ÷ 4 + RCL04 = STO16 STO12	062
5	RCL03 + RCL04 × RCL08 ÷ 2 = STO11 + RCL03 = × RCL08 ÷ 4 + RCL02 = STO10	090
6	RCL08 ÷ 2 = SUM09 SBR259 SUM14 STO15	104
7	÷ 2 + RCL05 = STO13 RCL03 + RCL16 × RCL08 ÷ 2 = STO11	125
8	SBR259 SUM14 SUM15	132
9	+ RCL05 = STO13 + RCL05 = ×RCL08 ÷ 2 + RCL04 = STO12	153
10	RCL03 + RCL16 × RCL08 = STO11 + RCL03 = × RCL08 ÷ 2 + RCL02 = STO10	179

11 RCL08 SUM01 RCL01 STO09 SBR259
SUM15   192

12 RCL04 − RCL16 = × RCL08 x^2 ÷ 6 + RCL10 =
STO02   210

13 RCL04 + 4 × RCL16 + RCL12 = × RCL08 ÷ 6 =
SUM03   229

14 RCL14   SUM15 ÷ 6 + RCL05 = × RCL08 =
SUM04   245

15 RCL15 ÷ 6 = SUM05   252

16 2nd Dsz 7012   RCL02   R/S   259

17 2 × RCL13 − 3 × RCL12 + 5 × RCL11 − 3 ×
RCL10 = × RCL08 = INV SBR   284

LRN

Contents of data registers

01 x_i 02 y_i 03 y_i' 04 y_i'' 05 y_i''' 06 x_n 07 $n-i$ 08 h
09 x   10 y, s   11y_i' 12 y_i'', r_2 13 y_i''' 14 $q_1 + q_2 + q_3$
15 $q_1 + 2q_2 + 2q_3 + q_4$ 16 r_1

Input/output

Press x_0 STO01 y_0 STO02 y_0' STO03 y_0'' STO04
        y_0''' STO05 x_n STO06   n STO07   RST   R/S

Display y_n

If y_n', y_n'', and y_n''' are required, they are obtained by pressing RCL03, RCL04, and RCL05.

Results appear in the table below for the input data

$x_0 = 0$ $y_0 = y_0' = y_0'' = y_0''' = 1$
$x_n = .5,$ 1.0,   1.5,   2.0
$n = 5,$ 10,   15,   20

Each value of n corresponds to the value of x_n directly above. The exact solution $y = e^x$ is shown for comparison.

x_n \ y_n	*exact*	*Runge-Kutta*
0.5	1.6487213	1.6487213
1.0	2.7182818	2.7182815
1.5	4.4816891	4.4816809
2.0	7.3890561	7.3890151

The same remarks about obtaining results after the first which were made in the first two sections apply here also. For example, after the value of y has been found at the point x = .5, we obtain the value of y at the point x = 1.0 by pressing 1 STO06 5 STO07 GTO012 R/S.

In practical applications equation (16) often appears in the simpler form

$$\frac{d^4y}{dx^4} = y^{IV} = f(x,y,y'') \tag{20}$$

in which the odd order derivatives are missing. A shorter Runge-Kutta program can be written for this case. The equations are

$$q_1 = hf(x_i, y_i, y_i'') \tag{21a}$$

$$r_1 = y_i'' + \frac{h}{2} y_i''' + \frac{h}{8} q_1 \tag{21b}$$

$$q_2 = hf\left(x_i + \frac{h}{2}, y_i + \frac{h}{2} y_i' + \frac{h^2}{8} y_i'', r_1\right) \tag{21c}$$

$$r_2 = y_i'' + hy_i''' + \frac{h}{2} q_2 \tag{21d}$$

$$s = y_i + hy_i' + \frac{h^2}{2} r_1 \tag{21e}$$

$$q_3 = hf(x_i + h, s, r_2) \tag{21f}$$

$$y_{i+1} = s + \frac{h^2}{6}(y_i'' - r_1) \qquad\qquad (21g)$$

$$y_{i+1}' = y_i + \frac{h}{6}(y_i'' + 4r_1 + r_2) \qquad\qquad (21h)$$

$$y_{i+1}'' = r_2 + \frac{h}{6}(q_1 - q_2) \qquad\qquad (21i)$$

$$y_{i+1}''' = y_i''' + \tfrac{1}{6}(q_1 + 4q_2 + q_3) \qquad\qquad (21j)$$

A program for the equation

$$\frac{d^4y}{dx^4} + 5\frac{d^2y}{dx^2} + 4y = 0$$

follows.

0	LRN	000
1	RCL06 − RCL01 = ÷ RCL07 = STO08	012
2	RCL04 STO11 RCL02 STO10 RCL01 STO09 SBR202 STO12 STO13	031
3	÷ 4 + RCL05 = × RCL08 ÷ 2 + RCL04 = STO14 STO11	050
4	RCL04 × RCL08 ÷ 4 + RCL03 = × RCL08 ÷ 2 + RCL02 = STO10	072
5	RCL08 ÷ 2 = SUM09 SBR202 INV SUM12 × 4 = SUM13	090
6	÷ 8 + RCL05 = × RCL08 + RCL04 = STO11	105
7	RCL14 × RCL08 ÷ 2 + RCL03 = × RCL08 + RCL02 = STO10	125
8	RCL08 SUM01 RCL01 STO09 SBR202 SUM13	138

9   RCL04 − RCL14 = ×RCL08 x^2 ÷ 6 + RCL10 =
STO02   156

10   RCL04 + 4 × RCL14 + RCL11 = × RCL08 ÷
6 = SUM03   175

11   RCL12 × RCL08 ÷ 6 + RCL11 = STO04   188

12   RCL13 ÷ 6 = SUM05   195

13   2nd Dsz 7012   RCL02   R/S   202

14   5 × RCL11 +/− − 4 × RCL10 = × RCL08 =
INV SBR   218

LRN

Contents of data registers

01 x_i 02 y_i 03 y_i' 04 y_i'' 05 y_i''' 06 x_n 07 $n-i$ 08 h
09 x   10 y, s   11 y'', r_2 12 $q_1 - q_2$ 13 $q_1 + 4q_2 + q_3$
14 r_1

The input/output procedure is the same as that given previously for the general fourth order equation. Results appear in the table below for the input data

$x_0 = 0$ $y_0 = 1$ $y_0' = y_0''' = 0$ $y_i'' = -1$
$x_n = .5,$ 1.0,   1.5,   2.0
$n = 5,$ 10,   15,   20

Each value of n corresponds to the value of x_n directly above. The exact solution y = cos x is shown for comparison.

x_n \\ y_n	exact	Runge-Kutta
0.5	.87758257	.87758263
1.0	.54030231	.54030256
1.5	.07073720	.07073767
2.0	−.41614684	−.41614625

5. Initial value problems and boundary value problems

In all of the problems that we have considered, all of the required conditions on y and its derivatives have been specified at one point (i.e. one value of the independent variable), which could be used as the starting point for the numerical evaluation. Any problem involving a first order differential equation is of this type, since there is only one condition to be satisfied. However, when the differential equation is of second or higher order, there are two or more conditions to be satisfied. If all of the conditions are specified at one point, the problem is known as an initial value problem. A problem in which conditions are specified at two points is known as a boundary value problem. The methods that we have considered apply directly to initial value problems. To solve a boundary value problem, an extension of the foregoing methods is necessary.

Second order differential equations. For a linear second order differential equation, it is possible to solve a boundary value problem by solving two initial value problems and then using superposition, that is linear interpolation. The easiest way to understand the method is to consider an example. Suppose that we require the solution of equation (9) which satisfies the boundary conditions

$$x = 0:\ y = 1 \qquad x = 1:\ y' = 0$$

and, in particular, we require the value of y at the point $x = 1$. We guess two values of y_0' (say 0 and 1) and run calculations from one of the programs of section 2, using the correct starting values $x_0 = 0$ and $y_0 = 1$ in both cases. Results from the Runge-Kutta program with $h = .1$ appear in the following table:

x_0	y_0	y_0'	x_n	y_n	y_n'
0	1	0	1	−1.573159	−7.864314
0	1	1	1	3.097131	4.194155

The value of y_0' which will make $y_n' = 0$ is

$$y_0' = \frac{7.864314}{7.864314 + 4.194155} = 0.6521818$$

The corresponding value of y at $x = 1$ is

$$y_n = -1.573159 + .6521818\,(3.097131 + 1.573159) = 1.472719$$

For optimum accuracy, the full intermediate results are stored and used in subsequent steps. Each result is rounded off when it is written down. We store the constants $-1.573159\ldots$ and $-7.864314\ldots$ in data registers 12 and 13, respectively. The constants $3.097131\ldots$ and $4.194155\ldots$ remain in data registers 02 and 03 after the program is run for the second time. Then the foregoing calculations become

$$1 - \text{RCL}03 \div \text{RCL}13 = \frac{1}{x}$$

which gives the result .6521818. With this result still in the display, we press

$$\times\,(\text{RCL}02 - \text{RCL}12) + \text{RCL}12 =$$

which gives the result 1.472719.

The final result is checked by running the program again, starting with the correct initial values of x_0, y_0, and y_0'. This leads to the results $y_n = 1.472719$ and $y_n' = 2.6 \cdot 10^{-11}$. These results show good agreement with the exact values, which are

$$y_n = \frac{e(8+3)-3}{4(2e-1)} = 1.472723 \qquad y_n' = 0$$

In this example we have made the interpolations manually after running the basic program. If results are required for a number of sets of input data, it may be advantageous to incorporate the interpolations into the program. This can easily be done when the TI-59 is used. It is not possible with all programs on the TI-58, because some of the programs take almost the full capacity of the calculator and do not leave much space for further manipulations.

This procedure is theoretically correct only for linear differential equations. For a boundary value problem involving a nonlinear differential equation, linear interpolation may be used to obtain a first estimate of the result. This must then be refined by trial and error. The secant method of chapter 2 can be combined with one of the methods of section 2.

Fourth order differential equations. For a fourth order differential equation, there are four conditions to be satisfied. If all of these are specified at one point, we have an initial value problem of the type considered in section 4. If three conditions are specified at one end of the interval and one condition is specified at the other end, we take $x = x_0$ at the end where three conditions are specified. The remaining boundary condition is handled in the same way as in the case of the second order differential equation just discussed. If two boundary conditions are specified at each end, the analysis is a little more complicated. The solution of the boundary value problem is obtained by superposition of three initial value solutions. The procedure will be illustrated by an example.

We require the solution of equation (19) which satisfies the boundary conditions

$$x = 0: \quad y = 1, \quad y' = 0 \qquad x = 1: \quad y'' = 0, \quad y''' = 0$$

and, in particular, we require the value of y at the point $x = 1$. The calculations are set out in the following table. The first three rows of figures are obtained by running the Runge-Kutta program of section 4 three times with the input data shown and $h = .1$. The fourth row is obtained by superposition of the first two and the fifth is obtained by superposition of the first and third. The sixth row is derived from the fourth and fifth.

x_0	y_0	y_0'	y_0''	y_0'''	x_n	y_n''	y_n'''
0	1	0	0	0	1	−2.679720	−6.808590
0	1	0	0	1	1	−.410171	−2.824022
0	1	0	1	0	1	−3.234221	−9.934331
0	1	0	0	1.708740	1	1.198350	0
0	1	0	−2.178232	0	1	−1.471890	0
0	1	0	−.977547	.941892	1	0	0

The final value of y_n cannot be obtained by further interpolations because we have not stored intermediate values of y_n. We run the program again, using the initial values in the last line of the table as input data. Then we find that $y_n = .702954$, which is the desired result. We also find that $y_n' = -.414191$, $y_n'' = -3.5 \cdot 10^{-12}$, and $y_n''' = -3.7 \cdot 10^{-11}$. The last two results provide a good check on the soundness of the analysis; these would be zero if the numerical calculations were exact.

Problems

Solve the differential equations 1 through 12 numerically at several points for the specified initial conditions. (Analytical solutions are given to make it easy to check the numerical results.)

1. $y' + 2y = x^2$ $\qquad$ $y(0) = \dfrac{1}{4}$ $\qquad$ $y = \dfrac{x^2}{2} - \dfrac{x}{2} + \dfrac{1}{4}$

2. $y' + y = \sin x$ $\qquad$ $y(0) = -\dfrac{1}{2}$ $\qquad$ $y = \dfrac{1}{2}(\sin x - \cos x)$

3. $y' + 2 \times y = x$ $\qquad$ $y(0) = 1$ $\qquad$ $y = \dfrac{1}{2}(1 - e^{-x^2})$

4. $y' + y = xy^2$ $\qquad$ $y(0) = 1$ $\qquad$ $y = \dfrac{1}{x+1}$

5. $y' + x^2(y - 3y^3) = 0$ $\qquad$ $y(0) = \dfrac{1}{2}$ $\qquad$ $y = \dfrac{1}{(e^{2x^3/3} + 3)^{1/2}}$

6. $y' + y \tan x = \sin 2x$ $\qquad$ $y(0) = 0$ $\qquad$ $y = 2 \cos x(1 - \cos x)$

7. $y' + (y^2 - 1)\tan x = 0$ $\qquad$ $y(0) = 3$ $\qquad$ $y = \dfrac{2 + \cos^2 x}{2 - \cos^2 x}$

8. $y' = \dfrac{y+1}{x+1}$ $\qquad$ $y(0) = 0$ $\qquad$ $y = x$

9. $y' = \dfrac{y^2 - 1}{x^2 - 1}$ $\qquad$ $y(2) = .8$ $\qquad$ $y = \dfrac{x+2}{2x+1}$

10. $xy' + y = xy$ $\qquad$ $y(1) = \dfrac{1}{2}$ $\qquad$ $y = \dfrac{e^{x-1}}{2x}$

11. Modify the Adams program of section 1 to obtain an iterative solution of the corrector equation (5c) as discussed under *Accuracy of numerical solutions* in section 1. Repeat the Adams solution of equation (4) with two iterative cycles in the solution of equation (5c), and verify the numerical results shown below. Compare these results with the ones given in the table of section 1 for the basic Adams method. Observe that in this problem the iterative process yields no improvement in accuracy; the error in solving equation (5c) approximately is of the same order as the inherent error in the equation itself.

x_n	.5	1.0	1.5	2.0
y_n	1.797443	3.436571	6.463401	11.778167

12. An analysis of the Adams method shows that the error of the corrected result is approximately $-\frac{19}{251}$ times the error of the predicted result. Therefore the equation

$$y_{i+1} = \frac{251}{270} y_{i+1}^C + \frac{19}{270} y_{i+1}^P = .93y_{i+1}^C + .07y_{i+1}^P$$

tends to balance the errors of the predictor and the corrector
and give a result which is more accurate than either. (The super-
scripts P and C refer to the predictor and the corrector, respectively.) The value of the corrector must be an accurate solution
of equation (5c). Revise the program of problem 11 to include
this equation, and use the new program to repeat the solution
of equation (4) and verify the results shown below. Observe that
the new results are better than the basic Adams results shown
in the table of section 1.

x_n	.5	1.0	1.5	2.0
y_n	1.797442	3.436563	6.463379	11.778116

APPENDIX

NUMERICAL
METHODS

The numerical concepts used in the first three chapters are essentially self-explanatory. In this appendix derivations are given for the three most important methods of the last two chapters: the Gauss method of numerical integration, and the Runge-Kutta and Adams methods of solving differential equations.

1. Gauss integration

The basic formula for numerical integration is

$$I = \int_a^b y \, dx = w_1 y_1 + w_2 y_2 + \ldots + w_n y_n \tag{1}$$

where the y_i's are the values of the function at n base points x_i and the w_i's are appropriate weighting factors. We represent the function y by a polynomial

$$y = a_0 + a_1 x + a_2 x^2 + \ldots \tag{2}$$

To obtain numerical results from equation (1), it is necessary to specify the values of x at the n base points at which the function is to be evaluated. One obvious possibility is to use uniformly spaced base points. Then the use of n points will determine the function y exactly and uniquely, provided that y is a polynomial of degree not greater than $n - 1$, and the numerical integration will be exact. Instead of arbitrarily choosing to place the base points $x_1, x_2, \ldots, x_n$ at equal intervals, we may choose to find the values of the x_i's which will lead to the most accurate numerical evaluation. If the x_i's are considered to be adjustable as well as the w_i's, we have 2n adjustable parameters, and it is possible to obtain an evaluation that will give exact results for a polynomial of degree $\leq 2n - 1$. This is the basic idea of Gauss integration.

Lagrange polynomials play a major part in the theory of Gauss integration. These are discussed in advanced calculus and have been considered briefly in chapter 1, section 5. To take advantage of the orthogonality properties of the Legendre polynomials, we change the interval of integration in equation (1), using limits -1 and 1 instead of a and b. We also change the independent variable to ξ, reserving the symbol x for the general interval a to b. After the analysis is completed on this basis, the results can easily be applied to the more general interval by using equation (9b) of chapter 4. The basic formula now becomes

$$I = \int_{-1}^{1} y \, d\xi = w_1 y_1 + w_2 y_2 + \ldots + w_n y_n \qquad (3)$$

The values of the ξ_i's and w_i's will now be found that lead to an exact numerical integration provided that y is a polynomial of degree not greater than $2n-1$. Let y be a polynomial of degree $2n - 1$. Then y may be written in the form

$$y = P_n(\xi) \, q_{n-1}(\xi) + r_{n-1}(\xi) \qquad (4)$$

where $P_n(\xi)$ is the Legendre polynomial of degree n, $q_{n-1}(\xi)$ is the quotient obtained by dividing $P_n(\xi)$ into y, and $r_{n-1}(\xi)$ is the remainder. $q_{n-1}(\xi)$ and $r_{n-1}(\xi)$ are polynomials of degree $n - 1$. Substitution of equation (4) into the middle member of equation (3) leads to

$$I = \int_{-1}^{1} P_n(\xi) \, q_{n-1}(\xi) + \int_{-1}^{1} r_{n-1}(\xi) \, d\xi$$

Since the function $q_{n-1}(\xi)$ is a polynomial of degree $n - 1$, it can be expressed as a linear combination of Legendre polynomials of degree not greater than $n - 1$. Each of these is orthogonal to $P_n(\xi)$ in the interval -1 to 1; therefore the first integral on the right side of the foregoing equation is zero, and it follows that

$$I = \int_{-1}^{1} r_{n-1}(\xi) \, d\xi \qquad (5)$$

Substitution of equation (4) into the last member of equation (3) leads to

$$I = \sum_{i=1}^{n} w_i [P_n(\xi_i) \, q_{n-1}(\xi_i) + r_{n-1}(\xi_i)] \qquad (6)$$

We want the numerical evaluation (6) to give exactly the same result as the exact expression (5). Since the latter expression is independent of $q_{n-1}(\xi)$, the former one must be also. This can be true if and only if

$$P_n(\xi_i) = 0 \qquad (7)$$

that is, the ξ_i's are the zeros of the Legendre polynomial $P_n(\xi)$.

We now have an equation for the ξ_i's, but we still need an equation for the w_i's. To obtain this we use the Lagrange interpolatory expression for y. The special case n = 4 has appeared previously as equation (17) of chapter 1. The general equation is

$$y = \sum_{i=1}^{n} \frac{(\xi - \xi_1)(\xi - \xi_2) \dots (\xi - \xi_{i-1})(\xi - \xi_{i+1}) \dots (\xi - \xi_n)}{(\xi_i - \xi_1)(\xi_i - \xi_2) \dots (\xi_i - \xi_{i-1})(\xi_i - \xi_{i+1}) \dots (\xi_i - \xi_n)} \, y_i \quad (8)$$

By integrating both sides of this equation between the limits -1 and 1, then comparing the result with equation (3) and matching coefficients of corresponding terms, we find that

$$w_i = \int_{-1}^{1} \frac{(\xi - \xi_1) \dots (\xi - \xi_{i-1})(\xi - \xi_{i+1}) \dots (\xi - \xi_n)}{(\xi_i - \xi_1) \dots (\xi_i - \xi_{i-1})(\xi_i - \xi_{i+1}) \dots (\xi_i - \xi_n)} \, d\xi$$

$$= \frac{1}{(\xi_i - \xi_1) \dots (\xi_i - \xi_{i-1})(\xi_i - \xi_{i+1}) \dots (\xi_i - \xi_n)}$$

$$\int_{-1}^{1} \frac{\displaystyle\prod_{j=1}^{n} (\xi - \xi_j)}{\xi - \xi_i} \, d\xi \quad (9)$$

It is clear that $P_n(\xi)$ can be expressed as

$$P_n(\xi) = c \prod_{j=1}^{n} (\xi - \xi_j)$$

where c is the coefficient of ξ^n and the ξ_j's are the roots of equation (7). It follows that

$$P'_n (\xi_i) = c(\xi_i - \xi_1) \cdots (\xi_i - \xi_{i-1})(\xi_i - \xi_{i+1}) \cdots (\xi_i - \xi_n)$$

Equation (9) now becomes

$$w_i = \frac{1}{P'_n (\xi_i)} \int_{-1}^{1} \frac{P_n(\xi)}{\xi - \xi_i} \, d\xi \quad (10)$$

To evaluate this integral we need Christoffel's summation formula (reference 6, page 101). This is

$$\frac{n}{\xi - \xi_i} [P_{n-1}(t) \, P_n(\xi) - P_n(t) \, P_{n-1}(\xi)] = [P_0(t) \, P_0(\xi)$$

$$+ \, 3P_1(t)P_1(\xi) + \dots + (2n - 1)P_{n-1}(t)P_{n-1}(\xi)] \quad (11)$$

We set $t = \xi_i$ and use equation (7). Then it follows that

$$\frac{P_n(\xi)}{\xi - \xi_i} = \frac{1}{nP_{n-1}(\xi_i)} [P_o(\xi_i)P_o(\xi) + 3P_1(\xi_i)P_1(\xi) + \ldots$$

$$+ (2n-1)P_{n-1}(\xi_i)P_{n-1}(\xi)] \quad (12)$$

We substitute equation (12) into the right side of (10). The integrals of all of the terms in brackets except the first are equal to zero, and we find that

$$w_i = \frac{2}{nP_{n-1}(\xi_i)P'_n(\xi_i)} \quad (13)$$

It follows from equations (15) of chapter 1 and equation (7) that

$$nP_{n-1}(\xi_i) = (1 - \xi_i^2)P'_n(\xi_i) \quad (14)$$

Equation (13) can be rewritten in either of the two final forms

$$w_i = \frac{2}{(1 - \xi_i^2)[P'_n(\xi_i)]^2} \quad (15)$$

or

$$w_i = \frac{2(1 - \xi_i^2)}{n^2[P_{n-1}(\xi_i)]^2} \quad (16)$$

The most convenient form depends upon the method which is used to compute $P_n(\xi)$. Equation (15) works very well with the method of chapter 1, section 5, since this method gives $P'_n(\xi)$.

We now have the desired equations to evaluate the Gauss coefficients. The ξ_i's are found from equation (7), and the w_i's are found from equation (15) or (16). Only half of the required ξ_i's and w_i's actually have to be calculated. Since each Legendre polynomial contains only even powers or only odd powers, the ξ_i's given by equation (7) occur in $\pm$ pairs. Also, the corresponding w_i's occur in positive pairs, since only squares of the parameters appear on the right side of equation (15). As a result it is sufficient to consider the $n/2$ positive values of ξ_i if n is even, or the $(n + 1)/2$ positive values (including zero) if n is odd. For $n = 1$ through 5, the evaluations can easily be made algebraically. The results are

$$n = 1 \qquad \xi_1 = w_1 \qquad = 2$$

$$n = 2 \qquad \xi_1 = \frac{1}{\sqrt{3}} \qquad w_1 = 1$$

$$n = 3 \qquad \xi_1 = 0 \qquad w_1 = \frac{8}{9} \qquad \xi_2 = \sqrt{\frac{3}{5}} \quad w_2 = \frac{5}{9}$$

$$n = 4 \qquad \xi_{1,2} = \left[\frac{1}{7}\left(3 \mp \sqrt{\frac{24}{5}}\right)\right]^{1/2} \qquad w_{1,2} = \frac{1}{6}\left(3 \pm \sqrt{\frac{5}{6}}\right)$$

$$n = 5 \qquad \xi_1 = 0 \qquad\qquad\qquad w_1 = \frac{128}{225}$$

$$\xi_{2,3} = \frac{1}{3}\left(5 \mp \sqrt{\frac{40}{7}}\right)^{1/2} \qquad w_{2,3} = \frac{1}{900}(322 \pm 13\sqrt{70})$$

For larger values of n, the best way to evaluate the Gauss coefficients is to write a program. The basic numerical procedures can be found in chapters 1 and 2. We shall use a program segment based upon chapter 1, section 5, to evaluate $P_n(\xi)$. We shall then find the root ξ_i by using the Newton–Raphson method of iteration discussed in chapter 2, section 2. The method of evaluating $P_n(\xi)$ of chapter 1 fits very well with the Newton–Raphson method because it gives $P'_n(\xi)$ as well as $P_n(\xi)$. The value of w_i will be found by using equation (15). There is one essential element which we do not yet have; an estimate of ξ_i is needed to start the iteration process. We can get this from the equation

$$\xi_i = \sin\left[\frac{\pi}{n}(i - .5)\right] \qquad \text{n even} \qquad i = 1,2,3,\ldots,\frac{n}{2} \tag{17a}$$

$$= \sin\left[\frac{\pi}{n}(i - 1)\right] \qquad \text{n odd} \qquad i = 1,2,3,\ldots,\frac{n+1}{2} \tag{17b}$$

The number of cycles necessary to obtain results accurate to the full extent of the calculator display is $i + 3$.

The program appears below. Line 1 stores n, the index of the Legendre polynomial. Line 2 calculates and stores the counter for an iterative Dsz loop. Lines 2 and 3 use equation (17) to obtain a preliminary estimate of ξ_i. Lines 4 to 7 constitute an outer Dsz loop which obtains an iterative solution of equation (7), using the Newton–Raphson method. Lines 5 and 6 constitute an inner Dsz loop which evaluates $P_n(\xi)$. This segment is essentially the same as the ones used

154

in chapter 1, section 5, with one exception. It is not necessary to make any provision for the case $n = 0$, since this case is meaningless. Line 8 evaluates w_i, using equation (15). Numerical results are identical to those given in chapter 4, section 2.

0	LRN	000
1	2nd Lbl A STO01 R/S	005
2	2nd Lbl B + 3 = STO05 − (RCL01 ÷ 2) INV 2nd Int − 3.5 =	026
3	× 2nd π ÷ RCL01 = 2nd Rad 2nd sin STO02	036
4	RCL01 STO04 0 STO03 1 STO00	046
5	× RCL00 + RCL02 × RCL03 = 2nd Exc 03	058
6	+/− + RCL02 × RCL03 = ÷ RCL00 = 2nd Op 20 2nd Dsz 4046	076
7	÷ RCL03 = INV SUM 02 2nd Dsz 5036 RCL02 R/S	090
8	2nd Lbl C $x^2 - 1 = \dfrac{1}{x} \times 2$ ÷ RCL03 x^2 = +/− R/S	106

Contents of data registers

00 1,2,3, ...   01 n   02 ξ 03 $P_{n-1}(\xi), P_n(\xi)$
04 n, n − 1, ... , 1   05 counter for iteration loop

Input/output

Press   n A   i B   C

Display ξ_i w_i

For a fixed value of n, the input instruction n A may be omitted for each value of i after the first.

It is theoretically possible to combine the foregoing program with the program for Gauss integration of chapter 4, section 2. The combined program would be self-contained, requiring no tabular input. Unfortunately this is totally impractical; the running time of a combined program is prohibitive. In practice the Gauss coefficients are obtained only once, either from the foregoing program or from a table.

2. Differential equations

The Runge–Kutta method. To derive the Runge–Kutta formulas, we start with equation (1) of chapter 5, which is

$$y' = f(x,y) \tag{18}$$

The Taylor series expansion of y is

$$y_{i+1} = y_i + hy_i' + \frac{h^2}{2} y_i'' \dots \tag{19}$$

where $h = x_{i+1} - x_i$. This may be rewritten as

$$y_{i+1} = y_i + hf_i + \frac{h^2}{2} (f_{xi} + f_i f_{yi}) + \dots \tag{20}$$

where $f_i = f(x_i, y_i)$ and the subscripts x and y denote partial derivatives. We assume an approximation of the form

$$y_{i+1} = y_i + \alpha_1 hf(x_i,y_i) + \alpha_2 hf(x_i + \beta_1 h, y_i + \beta_2 hf_i) \tag{21}$$

and proceed to determine the constants α_1, α_2, β_1, and β_2 so that a Taylor series expansion of the right side of equation (21) will agree with the expansion (20) through terms of second degree in h.

The Taylor series expansion of $f(x_i + \Delta_1, y_i + \Delta_2)$ is

$$f(x_i + \Delta_1, y_i + \Delta_2) = f_i + \Delta_1 f_{xi} + \Delta_2 f_i f_{yi} + \dots$$

By setting $\Delta_1 = \beta_1 h$, $\Delta_2 = \beta_2 h$, and substituting the result into the last term on the right side of equation (21), we find that

$$y_{i+1} = y_i + (\alpha_1 + \alpha_2)hf_i + \alpha_2 h^2 (\beta_1 f_{xi} + \beta_2 f_i f_{yi}) \tag{22}$$

By equating coefficients of corresponding terms on the right sides of equations (20) and (22), we find that

$$\alpha_1 + \alpha_2 = 1 \qquad \beta_1 = \beta_2 = \frac{1}{2\alpha_2}$$

There are only three equations for four unknowns, so we have some freedom in choosing the constants. The simplest equations are obtained by setting

$$\alpha_1 = \alpha_2 = \tfrac{1}{2} \qquad \beta_1 = \beta_2 = 1$$

Equation (21) now becomes

$$y_{i+1} = y_i + \tfrac{1}{2}(q_1 + q_2) \tag{23a}$$

where

$$q_1 = hf(x_i, y_i) \qquad q_2 = hf(x_i + h, y_i + q_1) \tag{23b,c}$$

More accurate formulas are obtained by considering higher order terms in the Taylor series. By considering terms through h^4, we obtain equations (2) of chapter 5. Derivations can be found in books on numerical analysis, such as reference 11, pages 191–199.

The Adams method. We shall give a very simple derivation of the Adams method; more sophisticated derivations can be found in books on numerical analysis. We start by rewriting equation (18) in integral form as

$$y_{i+1} = y_i + \int_{x_i}^{x_{i+1}} f[x, y(x)]\, dx = y_i + \int_{x_i}^{x_{i+1}} f(x)\, dx \tag{24}$$

The subsequent algebra can be simplified by taking the origin at the point $x = x_i$. This will not affect the generality of the results. Then equation (24) becomes

$$y_{i+1} = y_i + \int_0^h f(x)\, dx \tag{25}$$

We need an approximate expression for $f(x)$. We choose the cubic polynomial

$$f(x) = a_0 + a_1 x + a_2 x^2 + a_3 x^3 \tag{26}$$

Then equation (25) becomes

$$y_{i+1} = y_i + a_0h + \tfrac{1}{2}a_1h^2 + \tfrac{1}{3}a_2h^3 + \tfrac{1}{4}a_3h^4 \qquad (27)$$

We assume that values of y are available at the four points $x_i = 0$, $x_{i-1} = -h$, $x_{i-2} = -2h$, $x_{i-3} = -3h$. By fitting the polynomial (26) to these four points, we arrive at the set of simultaneous equations

$$f_i = a_0$$
$$f_{i-1} = a_0 - a_1h + a_2h^2 - a_3h^3$$
$$f_{i-2} = a_0 - 2a_1h + 4a_2h^2 - 8a_3h^3$$
$$f_{i-3} = a_0 - 3a_1h + 9a_2h^2 - 27a_3h^3$$

where we have written f for f(x). The solutions are

$$a_0 = f_i$$
$$a_1 = \frac{1}{h}\left(\frac{11}{6}f_i - 3f_{i-1} + \frac{3}{2}f_{i-2} - \frac{1}{3}f_{i-3}\right)$$
$$a_2 = \frac{1}{h^2}\left(f_i - \frac{5}{2}f_{i-1} + 2f_{i-2} - \frac{1}{2}f_{i-3}\right)$$
$$a_3 = \frac{1}{h^3}\left(\frac{1}{6}f_i - \frac{1}{2}f_{i-1} + \frac{1}{2}f_{i-2} - \frac{1}{6}f_{i-3}\right)$$

Substitution of these results into equation (27) leads to

$$y_{i+1} = y_i + \frac{h}{24}(55f_i - 59f_{i-1} + 37f_{i-2} - 9f_{i-3}) \qquad (28)$$

This is the predictor equation (5b) of chapter 5.

Equation (28) has been obtained by extrapolation. The more accurate corrector equation (5c) of chapter 5 is obtained by using values of f at the points $x_{i+1} = h$, $x_i = 0$, $x_{i-1} = -h$, $x_{i-2} = -2h$. The simultaneous equations are

$$f_{i+1} = a_0 + a_1h + a_2h^2 + a_3h^3$$
$$f_i = a_0$$
$$f_{i-1} = a_0 - a_1h + a_2h^2 - a_3h^3$$
$$f_{i-2} = a_0 - 2a_1h + 4a_2h^2 - 8a_3h^3$$

The solutions are

$$a_0 = f_i$$

$$a_1 = \frac{1}{h}\left(\frac{1}{3}f_{i+1} - \frac{1}{2}f_i - f_{i-1} + \frac{1}{6}f_{i-2}\right)$$

$$a_2 = \frac{1}{h^2}\left(\frac{1}{2}f_{i+1} - f_i + \frac{1}{2}f_{i-1}\right)$$

$$a_3 = \frac{1}{h^3}\left(\frac{1}{6}f_{i+1} - \frac{1}{2}f_i + \frac{1}{2}f_{i-1} - \frac{1}{6}f_{i-2}\right)$$

Substitution of these results into equation (27) leads to

$$y_{i+1} = y_i + \frac{h}{24}(9f_{i+1} + 19f_i - 5f_{i-1} + f_{i-2}) \qquad (29)$$

that is the desired result.

REFERENCES

162

References

1. Texas Instruments, Inc., *Personal Programming.* Dallas, Tex., 1977.

2. ———*TI Programmable 58/59 Master Library,* Dallas, Tex., 1977.

3. ABRAMOWITZ, M. AND I. A. STEGUN, *Handbook of Mathematical Functions.* National Bureau of Standards, Applied Mathematics Series 55. Washington, D.C.: U.S. Government Printing Office, 1964. (The first edition of this handbook contains a number of misprints. Most of these have been corrected in subsequent printings.)

4. National Bureau of Standards, Applied Mathematics Series 41, *Tables of the Error Function and its Derivatives* (2nd ed.), Washington, D.C.: U.S. Government Printing Office, 1954.

5. FRANKLIN, P., *A Treatise on Advanced Calculus.* Chapter 16, New York: Dover Publications, 1940.

6. MACROBERT, T. M., *Spherical Harmonics,* Chapter 5, (2nd ed.), New York: Dover Publications, 1948.

7. HANCOCK, H., *Elliptic Integrals,* pp. 69, 81. New York: Dover Publications, 1917.

8. TRANTER, C. J., *Integral Transforms in Mathematical Physics,* pp. 67–72 (2nd ed.), London: Methuen, 1956.

9. STROUD, A. H. AND D. SECREST, *Guassian Quadrature Formulas.* Englewood Cliffs, N.J.: Prentice-Hall, Inc., 1966.

10. BAUER, F. L., H. RUTISHAUSER, AND E. STIEFEL, "New Aspects in Numerical Quadrature," from *Proceedings of Symposia in Applied Mathematics,* 15, (1963), Providence, R.I.: American Mathematical Society, 199–218.

11. RALSTON, A., *A First Course in Numerical Analysis.* New York: McGraw-Hill, 1965.

12. GERALD, C. F., *Applied Numerical Analysis* (2nd ed.), Reading, Mass.: Addison-Wesley, 1978.

13. Texas Instruments, Inc., *Sourcebook for Programmable Calculators,* Dallas, Tex., 1978.

14. SNOVER, S. N. AND M. A. SPIKELL, *How to Program Your Programmable Calculator.* Englewood Cliffs, N.J.: Prentice-Hall, Inc., 1979.

SUGGESTED SOLUTIONS
TO SELECTED PROBLEMS

Chapter 1

1. (c) A program follows:

```
0  LRN                                                    000
1  STO01 × 5 − 1 = × RCL01 x² + (3 × RCL01)
   INV ln x − RCL01   2nd Rad 2nd cos = R/S               027
   LRN
```

3. A program follows:

```
0  LRN                                                    000
1  x ⇌ t   5 2nd x ≥ t 047   10 2nd x ≥ t 036
   15 2nd x ≥ t 025                                       015
2  x ⇌ t × .07 + .3 = R/S                                 025
3  x ⇌ t × .08 + .15 = R/S                                036
4  x ⇌ t × .09 + .05 = R/S                                047
5  x ⇌ t × .1 = R/S                                       053
   LRN
```

The input is n RST R/S, where n is the number of checks. The total charge is displayed.

5. (a) The general term is

$$\frac{1}{[n(n+1)(n+2)]^2} = \frac{1}{[n(2+3n+n^2)]^2} = \frac{1}{[n(2+n(3+n))]^2}$$

A program follows:

```
0  LRN                                                    000
1  STO01   0 STO02                                        005
```

$$2 \quad RCL01 + 3 = \times RCL01 + 2 = \times RCL01 = x^2 \frac{1}{x} \text{SUM02} \quad 024$$

```
3  2nd Dsz 1005   RCL02   R/S                             031
   LRN
```

The input is n RST R/S, where n is the number of terms considered. The partial sum is displayed. With n = 20, the result is 0.029901, which agrees with the analytical result.

(c) The nested format works well for this series. The best nested version is

$$S = 1 - \tfrac{1}{2}(\tfrac{1}{2} - \tfrac{1}{2}(\tfrac{1}{3} - \tfrac{1}{2}(\tfrac{1}{4} - \ldots$$

A program follows:

0 LRN   000

1 STO01 $+ 1 = \dfrac{1}{x}$ 006

2 $\div 2 +/- + \text{RCL01} \dfrac{1}{x} = \text{2nd Dsz 1006}$ R/S   019

LRN

The last entry in line 1 is the number at the extreme right of the nested equation. Line 2 is a Dsz loop which executes $n - 1$ cycles, summing n terms of the original series. The input is $n - 1$ RST R/S.

7. A program follows:

0 LRN   000
1 1 STO00   STO01   STO02   007
2 2nd $\pi \div 2 = y^x$ RCL00 $-$ RCL00 $\times$ RCL01 $=$
  $\times$ (RCL00 $+ 1$) $=$ 029
3 2nd Exc 02   STO01   2nd Op 20   RCL02
  R/S   GTO007   041
  LRN

The value of I_2 is obtained by pressing RST R/S. Subsequent results are found by pressing R/S. A slightly more efficient program follows:

0 LRN   000
1 1 STO00   STO01   005
2 2nd Exc 01 $\times$ RCL00 $+/-$
  $+ (\text{2nd } \pi \div 2)\, y^x \text{RCL00} = \times (\text{RCL00} + 1) =$ 029
3 2nd Op 20   R/S   GTO005   035
  LRN

8. For the first program, press RCL00. The current value of n is displayed. This also works for the second program, but the current value of x_n is lost when it is replaced by n in the display register, since x_n is not stored. Errors will then appear in subsequent terms of the sequence. The best procedure is to press 2nd Exc 00 and read the value of n. The contents of the display register and data register 00 are then returned to their original locations by again pressing 2nd Exc 00.

9. Using the last program for this sequence (the one with the Dsz loop), press 20 A 1 B 2 C. The result is x_{20}. It is not necessary

to repeat the entire calculation to obtain x_{21}. With x_{20} still in the display register, press C. The cycle will run once even though the data register 00 is empty, since the Dsz statement is at the end of the loop. The result is x_{21}. (It is possible to obtain the further results x_{22}, x_{23}, ... in the same way.)

11. In expanded form, the equation for the binomial coefficient is

$$\binom{p}{q} = \frac{p(p-1)(p-2) \cdot \cdot \cdot \cdot (p-q+1)}{q(q-1)(q-2) \cdot \cdot \cdot \cdot 1} \qquad p \geq q \geq 1$$
$$= 1 \qquad\qquad\qquad\qquad p \geq q = 0$$

A program appears below. The inverted Dsz loop of section 5 is used so the program will work when $q = 0$.

```
0   LRN                                                    000
1   2nd Lbl A    STO01    R/S                              005
2   2nd Lbl B    STO02    1 SUM02                          012
3   INV 2nd Dsz 2029 × RCL01 ÷ RCL02 = 2nd Op 31
    GTO012    R/S                                          030
    LRN
```

The program is run by pressing p A q B. The value of the binomial coefficient is displayed.

Chapter 2

4–6. Find the real roots first, then factor them out of the original equation and solve the resulting quadratic by elementary algebra to obtain the complex roots.

8, 9, 13. Use radians.

Chapter 3

2. A program appears below. Lines 2 through 7 are substantially equivalent to lines 1 through 6 of the program for $E_1(x)$ in section 2. Lines 8 and 9 constitute an inverted Dsz loop (chapter 1, section 5) which represents the recurrence formula. Two data registers are used in addition to those of the original program of section 2. Data register 00 contains the counter for the Dsz loop of lines 8 and 9, and data register 09 contains the index n-1 of the recurrence formula. (This n is of course not the same as the n of the original program.) After the program is punched into the calculator, the value of Euler's constant is inserted into

data register 02 by the procedure of section 2. Results are then obtained by pressing n A x B.

0	LRN	000
1	2nd Lbl A STO00 R/S	005
2	2nd Lbl B STO01 × 2.5 + 16 = 2nd Int STO03	020
3	0 STO04 STO06 STO08 1 STO05 STO07	
	STO09	034
4	2nd Op 24 RCL04 2nd Prd 06 RCL05 SUM06	044
5	RCL04 2nd Prd 05 RCL01 2nd Prd 07	052
6	RCL06 ÷ RCL05 x² × RCL07 = SUM08	
	2nd Dsz 3034	068
7	RCL08 ÷ RCL01 INV ln x − RCL01 ln x − RCL02 =	083
8	INV 2nd Dsz 0108 × RCL01 +/− + RCL01	

$$\text{INV ln } x \frac{1}{x} =$$ 099

9	÷ RCL09 = 2nd Op 29 GTO083 R/S	109
	LRN	

4. Either of the two following expansions may be used:

$$F(x) = xe^{-x^2}\left(1 + \frac{x^2}{3 \cdot 1!} + \frac{x^4}{5 \cdot 2!} + \ldots\right)$$

or

$$F(x) = x\left[1 - \frac{(2x^2)}{1 \cdot 3} + \frac{(2x^2)^2}{1 \cdot 3 \cdot 5} - \ldots\right]$$

If the first series is used, the program resembles the one of section 3. If the second series is used, the program resembles the one of problem 3. The second series leads to a shorter program.

5. The expansion shown is an asymptotic series. Proceeding from left to right, the first few terms decrease in absolute value. Later terms increase, and the series diverges. However, for large values of x, good results can be obtained by terminating the series after some intermediate number of terms. Successive partial sums oscillate about the true value of the function. Good results are obtained by taking ten terms and adding half the value of the eleventh term. This gives a result which is midway between an upper and a lower bound, and is not far from the true value. (This trick does not work with all alternating series.) A program follows. The input is x RST R/S R/S. The first R/S leads to the

result $xe^{x^2}\text{erfc } x$, which is needed to check the program. The second R/S gives erfc x.

```
0  LRN                                                        000
1  STO01   10 STO02   .5                                      008
2  ÷ RCL01 x² × (RCL02 − .5) +/− + 1 = 2nd Dsz 2008   028
3  ÷ 2nd π √x = R/S                                           033
4  ÷ RCL01 x² INV ln x ÷ RCL01 = R/S                         044
   LRN
```

6. The following substitutions may be used:
   (a) $x = b \sin \theta$ (b) $x = b \cos \theta$ (c) $x = b \tan \theta$ (d) $x = (a^2 \cos^2 \theta + b^2 \sin^2 \theta)^{1/2}$

8. We rewrite the equation in nested form as

$$H_p(x) = \frac{\dfrac{4}{\pi}\left(\dfrac{x}{2}\right)^{p+1}}{\dfrac{3}{2}\dfrac{5}{2}\cdots\left(p+\dfrac{1}{2}\right)}\left(1 - \frac{\left(\dfrac{x}{2}\right)^2}{\dfrac{3}{2}\left(p+\dfrac{3}{2}\right)}\left(1 - \frac{\left(\dfrac{x}{2}\right)^2}{\dfrac{5}{2}\left(p+\dfrac{5}{2}\right)}\left(1 - \cdots\right.\right.\right.$$

A program follows. It is constructed in exactly the same way as the program for $J_p(x)$ in section 6.

```
0  LRN                                                            000
1  2nd Lbl A   STO02   R/S                                        005
2  2nd Lbl B ÷ 2 = STO01 × 4 + 4 = 2nd Int   STO03   1  021
3  × RCL01 x² ÷ (RCL03 + .5) ÷ (RCL02 + RCL03
   + .5) +/− + 1 = 2nd Dsz 3021                                   052
4  2nd Op 22 × RCL01 yˣ RCL02 × (RCL02 + .5)                      068
5  ÷ (RCL02 + .5) = 2nd Dsz 2068 × 4 ÷ 2nd π = R/S   087
   LRN
```

Chapter 4

9. Integrate by parts to show that

$$\int_0^{\pi/2} \ln \sin x \, dx = -\int_0^{\pi/2} \frac{x \, dx}{\tan x}$$

The new integral has already been evaluated in section 2.

10. By writing $\pi - x$ for x, show that

$$\int_0^\pi x \ln \sin x \, dx = \frac{\pi}{2} \int_0^\pi \ln \sin x \, dx = \pi \int_0^{\pi/2} \ln \sin x \, dx$$

Then use the result of problem 9.

11–13. Gauss-Chebyshev integration works very well for these three intergals.

16. We observe that

$$\int_0^\infty \frac{x \, dx}{e^{\alpha x} - 1} = \frac{1}{\alpha^2} \int_0^\infty \frac{x \, dx}{e^x - 1}$$

The desired results now follow from problem 15.

17. A numerical evaluation is not necessary; we observe that

$$\int_0^\infty \frac{x \, dx}{e^x + 1} = \int_0^\infty \frac{x \, dx}{e^x - 1} - \int_0^\infty \frac{2x \, dx}{e^{2x} - 1} = \frac{1}{2} \int_0^\infty \frac{x \, dx}{e^x - 1}$$

The desired result now follows from problem 15.

18. This integral can be evaluated numerically as it stands, since it is proper. However, the process converges very slowly. It is preferable to write $e^{-x/2}$ for x, then use the result of problem 15.

19. This integral can be evaluated by writing tan x for x, but the resulting program has a long running time because of a long subroutine and slow convergence. It is preferable to start with the elementary identity

$$\int_0^\infty \left[\frac{1}{e^x - 1} - \frac{1}{x(x + 1)} \right] dx = \left\{ \ln \left[\frac{x + 1}{x} (1 - e^{-x}) \right] \right\}_0^\infty = 0$$

The desired integral now becomes

$$I = \int_0^\infty \left(\frac{1}{1 + x} - e^{-x} \right) \frac{dx}{x}$$

We break the interval at the point $x = 1$ and write $1/x$ for x in the second of the new integrals. This leads to

$$I = \int_0^1 \left(1 - e^{-x} - e^{-1/x} \right) \frac{dx}{x}$$

which is well suited to numerical integration.

Chapter 5

11. The first 12 lines of the program are identical to the corresponding lines of the original Adams program of section 1, except that the statement SBR201 is changed to SBR215 in lines 2, 4, 5, 6, and 10. Lines 13 through 17 are modified as shown below. Line 13 stores the counter 2 for a little Dsz loop inside the Adams loop, which iterates the solution to equation (5c). The data register 00 is used, since this is empty after the Runge-Kutta loop of lines 2 through 9 is completed. Lines 14 and 15 of the original program are interchanged. The new line 14 is the iterative loop which solves equation (5c). The new line 15 shifts the contents of the data registers in preparation for the next cycle. Line 16 completes the Adams loop, and line 17 is the function subroutine. With the new arrangment of steps, it is necessary to store f_{i+1}. This is done in data register 14. The input/output operation is identical to that of the original program.

13	RCL05 SUM01 SUM06 2 STO00	174
14	SBR215 STO14 × 3 ÷ 8 + RCL13 +	
	RCL02 = STO07 2nd Dsz 0174 STO02	198
15	RCL14 2nd Exc 12 2nd Exc 11	
	2nd Exc 10 STO09	208
16	2nd Dsz 4114 RCL02 R/S	215
17	RCL06 + RCL07 = × RCL05 = INV SBR	226

12. The first 12 lines of the program are identical to the corresponding lines of the original Adams program of section 1, except that the statement SBR201 is changed to SBR229 in lines 2, 4, 5, 6, and 10. Lines 13 through 17 of the original program become the new lines 13 through 18 shown below. The parameters f_{i+1} and y_{i+1}^{P} are stored in data registers 14 and 15, respectively. The input/output operation is identical to that of the original program.

13	STO15 RCL05 SUM01 SUM06	
	2 STO00	176
14	SBR229 STO14 × 3 ÷ 8 + RCL13 +	
	RCL02 = STO07 2nd Dsz 0176	198
15	× .93 + RCL15 × .07 = STO02	212
16	RCL14 2nd Exc 12 2nd Exc 11	
	2nd Exc 10 STO09	222
17	2nd Dsz 4114 RCL02 R/S	229
18	RCL06 + RCL07 = × RCL05 = INV SBR	240

INDEX

M

N

O

P

R

S

U